I0815239

If you've ever seen the royals wave from the balcony of Buckingham Palace after a wedding (or as they call it, a pre-divorce), then you're familiar with the Queen Victoria Memorial, honouring Queen Victoria. It's the giant statue topped by a gilt bronze woman with wings looming over the tourists from the centre of the roundabout. The woman is Winged Victory. She stands there like the bride atop the wedding cake of colonialism. These days her pool provides a place for drunken soccer hooligans in plastic crowns to pee, but there was a time when she represented the most feared nation on earth—the America of her day. She reminds us of a time when the sun never set on the British Empire and the Commonwealth was a lot less common and much wealthier. And Newfoundland was Winged Victory's oldest colony. Newfoundland was the very first souvenir brought home by a tourist.

To the side, you'll find the Dominion Gates. They're made of pillars dedicated to the conquests that made up Victoria's empire. One of these pillars is emblazoned with a wreath bearing the name "Canada." Another reads "Newfoundland." Back when the memorial was unveiled in 1911, these two nations held equal status. Who would have thought that one pillar would eventually eat the other? But this was not an invasion. Not one shot was fired. Even back then, Canadians didn't like guns. Like Canadians, Newfoundlanders were so polite that when someone tried to take away our sovereignty, we just said, "Oh, did you want this land? Sorry. Didn't know. Go ahead. I'll just swim around until you're done with it."

In 1934, Newfoundland became the only dominion to give up self-government. We are the only country to ever vote itself out of existence. The only one in history to close up shop. To retire. Not to be conquered, but to tap out and submit. Never in history had a nation decided to sell the place and enjoy retired life on a pension of transfer payments. We surrendered. But why? How?

Newfoundland always seemed to be an oddity. When you look at a map, you'll see my rocky island homeland just off the Canadian coast, looking like a puzzle piece that didn't quite fit. But I guess you can make anything fit if you jam it in and crack off a bit here and there. The Beothuk were the Indigenous inhabitants of the island. They became extinct when the last of their people, a woman named Shanawdithit, died in St. John's in 1829. The official cause of her death was tuberculosis, but I always think of it as "complications from a severe case of colonialism."

The first Europeans to visit Newfoundland, the Vikings, came around AD 1000. Leif Erikson left Iceland and found our shores using the time-honoured exploration tactic of "row until you hit something." The Vikings thought they had discovered paradise. Only someone from a place called Iceland would think of Newfoundland as a vacation getaway. Leif Erikson settled in what is now known as L'Anse aux Meadows on the tip of Newfoundland's Northern Peninsula. But he called the rocky island Vinland, or "Wineland," after the grapevines he found there. To be clear, there are no grapes in Newfoundland. But some historians think that Leif may have been referring to blueberries or cranberries. Or maybe he knew that one day his discovery would boast the highest concentration of bars per capita in Canada. Not because Newfoundland is the Miami Beach of the north. We have that many bars because you have to be either crazy or drunk to make it through a Newfoundland winter. Luckily, Leif was both.

After a freezing wet snowy winter, Leif set sail for home and told all the other Vikings in Iceland and Greenland about the beautiful, warm, inviting place he had found. Leif had not only discovered the new world—he invented tourism. He never returned, but he did manage to convince his brother, Thorvald, to visit Vinland the next year.

LEIF

Oh, you must go to Vinland. It's lovely this time of year.

THORVALD

I've been meaning to take the kids somewhere nice. What is it like?

LEIF

Oh, it's great. So warm. And the beaches are amazing.

THORVALD

They're not rocky beaches, are they?

LEIF

No! No. Island life! Beautiful sandy beaches. Chill. I mean, reeeeeally chill. Kick back and read a saga. Plus, it's all-inclusive.

THORVALD

What does that mean?

LEIF

The drinks are included. The wine is free. That's why it's called Vinland.

THORVALD

How's the food? I'm not picky, just as long as it's not fish.

LEIF

Look, I'm booking up. It's already Skerpla. Come Heyannir, the longhouses will be fully booked and I'll only have sod huts available.

THORVALD

Okay. I really appreciate this. Wait. Why aren't *you* going?

LEIF

No reason.

And so Thorvald made the trip to Newfoundland—where he died. This is the first example of a developer lying about a time-share. But today, Leif's resort lives on and you can visit a national historic site built among the remains of Viking sod longhouses. You can even interact with summer students dressed as Vikings and hear authentic Viking sayings like "What are ya at there, buddy? You must be from Ontario, is ya? I got a cousin Gord up there. You don't know him, do ya?"

Newfoundland, a place that not even a Viking could survive, would be left alone for about five hundred years. Except of course by the Indigenous people, who had no trouble at all surviving the winter, spring, summer or fall. The only thing that could ruin things for them was more Europeans. And if history can teach us anything, it's that there are always more Europeans.

In 1497, Newfoundland was "discovered" by Italian explorer Giovanni Caboto (or John Cabot as he became known, because even in 1497, white people refused to learn how to pronounce foreign names properly). He was the very first "come from away." Like Leif, he wasn't so much a brilliant explorer as a terrible navigator. He was really looking for a faster route to Asia. In today's terms that would be like trying to fly from St. John's to Vancouver but landing on P.E.I. and calling it a success. So, pretty much like any standard Air Canada flight.

Cabot didn't encounter the Beothuk, but he did see evidence of fishing nets and a campsite, indications that people certainly lived there. I assume that the Beothuk, seeing Cabot's ships and being sensible, probably did what anyone would do when missionaries or salespeople ring your doorbell. Turn out the lights and pretend nobody is home until they go away.

CABOT

Hi. Do you live here? My name is Giovanni and I was wondering if you've heard about—

BEOTHUK

Yeah. Look, it's a bad time.

CABOT

It'll just take a minute. I'm just going door to door in the neighbourhood and asking how happy people are with their service.

BEOTHUK

What service?

CABOT

Your nation? Ruler? King and/or queen? Whatever you're into.

BEOTHUK

We don't really have any of that.

CABOT

Oh, great. Would you consider switching to colonialism? We have a great deal on now. Free installation.

BEOTHUK

We're not really interested.

CABOT

This deal won't last. It's a special Discovery Day promotion.

BEOTHUK

What discovery?

CABOT

This place! Newfoundland!

BEOTHUK

You mean Old-always-here-land? Look, I don't mean to be rude but I'm in the middle of catching a salmon, so . . .

CABOT

No worries. I'll just stay here forever and wait. I love Asia.

BEOTHUK

Where?

For a while, Newfoundland was a bit of a free-for-all. The Basques and the Portuguese fished alongside the English in a sort of colonial throuple. That all changed in 1583, when Sir Humphrey Gilbert arrived in Newfoundland to claim it for Queen Elizabeth I. (As with the *Godfather* movies, I prefer the sequel, Queen Elizabeth II.) The fishermen who were already living there didn't much like the idea of someone being all judgy and planting a flag and ruining their whole vibe. Gilbert was a member of

Parliament at the time, so when he showed up in Newfoundland, he became the first politician in North America to get a door slammed in his face. When he planted a flag, he didn't just claim dibs on the fishing grounds. He founded the British Empire, and Newfoundland became its first colony. Meanwhile, the Beothuk, peeking through the brush, looked at one another and said, "I told you they were serious about the tariffs."

On the way back, Gilbert's convoy encountered a storm and, being a politician, he refused to listen to any advice from the more seasoned sailors on board his ship. His ship soon sank, taking Gilbert with it. This was the first North American example of a politician not knowing what he was talking about. His famous last words were, "We are as near to heaven by sea as by land." And, I assume he soon found out, as near to hell.

It didn't matter if you were John Cabot, Thorvald Erikson or Sir Humphrey Gilbert. It seemed that if you arrived in a boat, you were likely leaving Newfoundland in a box. But still they came, in literal boatloads. It turns out the Newfoundland cod fishery was the greatest in the world, and desperate people would risk everything to be a part of it. Cod was the crypto of its day. And some of those desperate people were Critches.

I had always wondered where my family came from. But my family never liked to look back. I once asked my father if he would like to research our family tree. "Good

God," he said, sucking back a cup of tea from his regular perch at the kitchen table. "Why in the world would you want to do that? People spend all that money to find out where they came from and then they spend twice as much to cover it all up again." This made me a little worried. What did he know that I didn't?

You could say that our family tree had been over-watered. My great-great-great-grandfather was a fisherman who drowned. My great-great-grandfather was also a fisherman who drowned. My great-grandfather broke the fishing tradition of the Critches. He was a whaler. He was washed overboard by an errant wave and (surprise!) drowned. At least my family saved a lot of money on burial costs. My father, orphaned at the age of six, was the first in his line to avoid the water and the first Critch male in generations to live past forty. He became a journalist and lived to the ripe old age of ninety-three. No wonder he didn't want to look back. Nothing good lay that way. Hope lay in the other direction.

When I did finally research our family history, I learned that it was that same hope that brought the Critches to Newfoundland. New world. New name. New life. New hope. They came from near Dartmouth in Devon, England. It's a pretty town of colourful houses that hug the hillside next to a well-protected harbour. And overlooking the town is Greenway House. It's almost exactly like the St. John's I grew up in. Today, tourists flock there because it was the home of the queen of mystery novels, Agatha Christie. But long before that, it was the birthplace and family home of Sir Humphrey Gilbert. It's no wonder that the Critches ended up in Newfoundland. The man who claimed it for England was their neighbour.

Two hours away is the town of Poole, home to the merchants who controlled the Newfoundland fishery. Codfish financed all the Georgian mansions you see there today. Even the church there is built with beams of Newfoundland pine. The main drag is still called Newfoundland Drive. At the end of it you would have found the Newfoundland Inn, where the men showed up hoping to be picked as crew. I stood on the very dock where my ancestors would have left their lives behind. It was on that spot that they exchanged their cold, dreary existence spent risking their lives on the water for new ones where they would risk their lives on the water until the end of their cold, dreary existence.

In 1922, my father was born a British subject who would never see Europe. He later became a Canadian without ever having left his hometown. It didn't matter if it was to the prime minister of the United Kingdom or the prime minister of Canada, he still had to pay his taxes. Canadian and British money had the same monarch on it, but it didn't matter what money looked like if you didn't have any.

The year 1949 wasn't the first time Newfoundland had flirted with joining Canada. During the election of 1869, Newfoundland's government was pro-Confederation. A deal was even close to being completed. But the fiercely anti-confederate opposition party knew that the voters could be swayed by their hearts more than their pockets. A popular song warned against Confederation.

Would you barter the right that your fathers have won?
Your freedom transmitted from father to son?
For a few thousand dollars Canadian gold
Don't let it be said that our birthright was sold.

Men, hurrah for our own native Isle, Newfoundland,
Not a stranger shall hold one inch of its strand;
Her face turns to Britain, her back to the Gulf,
Come near at your peril, Canadian Wolf!

A foreign country wanting to absorb their neighbour. Public opposition leading to loud cries of patriotism. Sound familiar? The more things change, the more they stay the same. But Newfoundlanders all agreed that they wanted nothing to do with Canada, and nothing could change that. And then there was a bank crash. Newfoundland stood on the verge of bankruptcy, and all of a sudden Canada looked pretty darn good! But, now completely broke, Newfoundland wasn't as attractive as it had been before. The deal fizzled. Newfoundland had played hard to get, and Canada had moved on.

Things got worse from there when World War I broke out. At first, war was bad for the world but good for Newfoundland. War meant that fewer countries were fishing, which drove up the price of fish. The forestry and mining industries benefited from the wartime demand for lumber and iron ore, and the Newfoundland government found itself with its first financial surplus in years. But there was a much heavier price to pay. On July 1, 1916, the first day of the Battle of the Somme, the Newfoundland Regiment made a tragic sacrifice. Some eight hundred Newfoundlanders fought at the Battle of Beaumont-Hamel. The next day, only sixty-eight answered the roll call. The Newfoundland Regiment had been all but wiped out, and with it a generation of future business leaders and politicians.

In all, Newfoundland spent about $35 million on the war. And that was for a country with a population of just 250,000. The interest payments on the public debt alone were a quarter of our national revenue. And when peacetime came, the price of fish and the demand for natural resources dropped. As we would say in Newfoundland, "The arse was out of 'er." Things had gone very wrong. By the time the Great Depression hit the rest of the world in 1929, Newfoundland was already too depressed to even get out of bed. We had to borrow money from the United

Kingdom (Mom and Dad) to repay the war debt we incurred defending the United Kingdom. They were happy to help, with one condition: that we give up our self-governance. They'd decided we couldn't handle having a place of our own. They wanted us to move back in with our parents.

And so, on February 16, 1934, to save us from bankruptcy, Newfoundland's responsible government voted itself out of existence. A country that once had its own prime minister would be run by a bunch of unelected Brits. And once the debt had been repaid, they couldn't wait to get rid of us. But who would want us?

In 1946, a National Convention was held to decide our future. At the time, my father, the first literate Critch, was a reporter with the local newspaper, the *Daily News*, where he covered the great event. The debate was less political discourse and more of an all-out brawl. Newfoundlanders would be given three options on the ballot: responsible government, commission rule or Confederation. The first option: get our own place again. The second: move back in with Mom and Dad. The third? An arranged marriage with Canada.

The third option is the one Britain wanted us to choose. They kept selling us: "Canada is a very nice boy. And you love the outdoors. He's not flashy like the States but he's dependable. Would it kill you to have dinner once?!?"

The self-government side was led by Maj. Peter Cashin. He gave a stirring speech at the National Convention. "I say to you," he said, "that there is in operation at the present time a conspiracy to sell, and I use the word 'sell' advisedly, this country to the Dominion of Canada. Watch, in particular, the attractive bait which will be held out to lure our country into the Canadian mousetrap. Listen to their flowery sales talk which will be offered to you; telling Newfoundlanders they're a lost people, that our only hope, our only salvation, lies in following a new Moses into the promised land across the Cabot Strait."

That "new Moses" hoping to "sell" his country was Joey Smallwood, a former pig farmer turned politician, if there's any real difference between the two professions. Being a pig farmer, he had no problem slinging crap, so politics came naturally to him.

For many folks like my ancestors, life had not changed all that much from the one they fled in England. One of the key pieces of bait that got the fishermen on the hook was the "baby bonus," or the Canadian Family Allowance. Mothers of school-age children would receive a tax-free sum every month. And that gave Smallwood an edge. Yes, Joey Smallwood might be a Judas. But he was a Judas with a cheque, and it was hard to argue with a dollar in your pocket.

Smallwood's side won with just 52 percent of the vote. He had convinced his own people to surrender their country voluntarily, without a single shot being fired. Newfoundland became a Canadian province at 11:59 p.m. on March 31, 1949. The marriage was made official a few seconds before midnight because Smallwood didn't want Confederation happening on April Fool's Day.

True to Canada's word, the baby bonus cheques came. Over fifty thousand mothers were paid nearly $10 million in that first year alone as Canadians. Each year after, their children grew taller and fatter and healthier. But they would never again be Newfoundlanders. They were Canadians.

Not everyone was happy. Generations of Newfoundlanders were exiled overnight without ever having left their homes. Losing your country makes you a stranger in your own house. Yes, the hills and bays looked the same, but they had become "somewhere else" overnight. Many longed for a home they could never go back to but had never left. They wore black armbands and flew their flags at half-mast. It turns out that you don't have to leave a place to miss it. And you don't have to misplace something to lose it.

For the generations since, the young people who grew up as Canadians, there could be no other way. No marriage is perfect. But for over seventy-five years now, Newfoundlanders and Labradorians have leaned on Canada in the hard times. And, lately, in the good times, we have helped drive the economy with our offshore oil and hydroelectricity projects. I'm a proud Canadian. And despite the Vikings' and Cabot's and Sir Humphrey Gilbert's best efforts, Newfoundland and Labrador has finally found its forever home. But there are still echoes of what might have been.

July 1 is Canada Day, and across the provinces and territories Canadians put aside their differences to celebrate their country with fireworks and barbecues. But in Newfoundland and Labrador, July 1 is still Memorial Day. In the morning we remember the Battle of Beaumont-Hamel and the hundreds of lives lost in that faraway field. We gather at the National War Memorial in downtown St. John's to lay wreaths at the Tomb of the Unknown Soldier. He was born in Newfoundland, died in France fighting for England and now rests forevermore in Canada, a country he never knew. The war he fought in, and the price Newfoundlanders paid to fight it, led to the demise of the country he loved. And so the place he rests is much more than a memorial to a war. In some ways, it is a tombstone for a country.

And so, on July 1, Memorial Day, we still sing the old Newfoundland anthem.

As loved our fathers, so we love
Where once they stood we stand
Their prayer we raise to heav'n above
God guard thee, Newfoundland.

And then, at noon on July 1, Canada Day, the past remembered, we fire up the barbecues and light the fireworks and sing a new song.

O Canada, we stand on guard for thee.

After all, hope lies in the future.

A Letter from the Desk of the 45th and 47th President of the United States

They're the same guy, which is remarkable, isn't it? It really is. A double presidency with a different guy in between. I'm like the bread in a ham sandwich and the pig is Joe Biden. And when you take into account that Sleepy Joe stole the election when he became the forty-sixth president, it's incredible. If the lying Democrats—they're a disaster, the biggest, let's be honest—hadn't stolen that election, then I would have been the forty-sixth, too. Which, they tell me, has never been done. A three-timer. So, for now, I'm just a two-timer. And people say that, believe me. I hear them. I walk down the street and I hear people saying, "There goes Donald Trump, the two-timer." You can't do three terms, they tell me, but that could change. We are looking into that, right now. I have the very best people. And they are looking into *the possibility of a third term. They tell me there are ways it could be done. And we are looking at those ways very closely, let me tell you.*

Oh, Canada,

My darling, why haven't you written back? Didn't you get my other letters or are your postal workers on strike again? Why won't you accept my proposal? I want to make you my 51st state. The state of marriage. United in marriage and united in states. I can't stop thinking of you. Your Great Lakes full of crystal-clear water that would quench my never-ending thirst. How I long to explore your lush interior. Not only do I want to call you mine, but I also want to mine you. And you can't spell minerals without "mine."

Your melting Arctic is slowly opening her trade routes like a blossoming flower. Let me become your honeybee. Oh, how I want to fertilize you. Don't make me sting you. Give yourself willingly to the buzzing exploration of a honeybee's lapping tongue. I cannot help but dream of your dark, wet, chocolatey oil dripping down your pipeline, bringing sweet salvation like the delicious Diet Coke delivered to my waiting lips from a straw.

A plastic straw. Not the paper ones. They're a disaster. You get maybe one or two sucks and they just fall apart, am I right? They evaporate and you're left drinking out of a can like a caveman. It's horrible. You get the Diet Coke all over your pants, which is worse if you're golfing and wearing your khaki pants, which we wear a lot at Mar-a-Lago because we do the sports there.

I got a hole-in-one on every hole, which is really an eighteen-in-one, if you think about it. But you do the sports in your khaki pants and if you get the Diet Coke on your lap, people might think you had an accident and then the fake news, the lying leftists at CNN, will say "Trump has wee-wee on his pants," and it's all because of a paper straw. We've all been there.

And paper straws are also very dangerous because if you have a spill, you could slip and fall like Biden. Did you see him? Trying to walk up the stairs of Air Force One and falling down? He was senile and they covered it up and we are going to get to the bottom of it, and also Hunter's laptop. Let's not forget that. But mostly Joe Biden.

That's how much I love you, Canada. I'm falling for you like Joe Biden falling up the stairs.

I wanted to live inside you from the moment I first learned about you—during Vietnam when I was desperately trying to avoid the draft. Lucky for both of us, I suddenly developed a lifelong problem with bone spurs. Before then, I didn't know that Canada was a real place. I always assumed it was a fairy-tale fantasyland like Narnia, Atlantis or Finland. But now, Canada, it's you who should be drafted. Drafted into becoming the 51st state. I know that you're still mad after seeing my texts with Greenland. But I was just using her to make you jealous. Greenland means nothing to me anymore.

Although she is in a very strategic location that would be tremendous for defence and she has so many incredible minerals. And the oil on her! Are you kidding me? If I could just get under that ice sheet and get my hands on her . . .

I promise to stop seeing Greenland if you'll have me. You are my only desire. My true love. I want no one else but you. Unless you think you'd be into a ménage à trois thing. I mean, you are half French, after all. And I bet some crazy stuff goes down backstage at those Cirque du Soleil shows. I'm just saying, I'd be cool with it if you'd like to explore the whole Greenland thing with me a little more. Maybe we can get together sometime? Have you considered polyamory?

Where did I go wrong? You've been so cold lately, which I guess is to be expected from such a snowy place, but still. Why do I do this to myself? You're the only woman I've ever loved. No one could ever compare to you.

But I could probably do a lot better than you, let me tell ya. I could have any country I want, let's be honest. Any country we have ever made an advance towards has welcomed us with open arms. Well, except maybe Cuba. Or Korea. Or Vietnam. Or Iraq. Or Afghanistan. Or Greenland. But we could have pretty much anyone else we wanted.

And yet you are playing hard to get. Which doesn't work, by the way. It only attracts me even more. Nothing turns me on more than someone telling me they don't want me. Maybe that's why I'm constantly aroused.

I'm like the skunk in the Looney Tunes cartoons who keeps trying to seduce that cat with the white paint stripe on her back. I think his name is Pepé Le Pew. Or Emmanuel Macron. Or maybe Emmanuel Le Pew. Pepé Macron? One is the president of France, the other is a cartoon skunk, they're easy to confuse, but it's one of those. Pepé Le Pew! That's it. You don't see him much anymore. They say he was cancelled by the left. He's like a cartoon skunk Scott Baio. Sad.

The radical left won't hire him because he's MAGA. Or so Jon Voight tells me. He's my eyes and ears in Hollywood. Kid Rock is my guy for music. But Jon Voight is my guy for acting. We have a lot in common. We both have hot daughters.

Anyway, the skunk hugs and squeezes the cat and kisses her paw and no matter how many times she says no, the skunk continues to pursue her. That's how I love you, Canada. Like a horny skunk, blissfully unaware of consent.

It's okay. Play hard to get. I've always liked cold women.

Melania and I were only able to have Barron because she had frozen her eggs. She didn't even need to use a fridge. She only had to think of being with me and the thought of it chilled her to the bone. Or at least I assume that's what happened. I'd ask her, but she stopped talking to me in 2016. That's how I like my women. As cold as they are hot. Emotionally distant enough that they don't talk to me, and passionless enough that they won't get up and leave me.

That's why I love you, Canada. You are the only woman who can't leave me. We are bound geographically. We were meant to be. I love you, Canada, and I would marry you—but I would prefer to have you as a side piece. Don't get me wrong. I want so much more than I had with Stormy Daniels, but I would still require an NDA. I'm offering a classy, mutually beneficial arrangement where I protect you and give you money, and in return I get to totally screw you. Canada, I am asking you to be my sugar baby, quite frankly.

Like I told your current husband, Mark Carney, when he came to the White House, "A border is just an imaginary line drawn by some guy. Somebody drew that line many years ago with, like, a ruler—just a straight line right across the top of the country." A border is meaningless, unless it's the Mexican border, and in that case, we need a wall, we really do. A big, beautiful wall and Mexico is gonna pay for it, let me tell ya. But when it comes to Canada, borders are just imaginary lines. You can't keep people out. Unless it's Mar-a-Lago. Then you need a big fence to keep people out. Maybe even an electric one. Or you know what would be great? A gas-powered electric fence. Could we do that? That'd be marvellous, wouldn't it? I think we could. We'll look into that. But other than Mexico and Mar-a-Lago, borders are just pretend.

We don't need a border. After all, we are already sleeping together, Canada. Pierre Elliott Trudeau, the father of the last governor of Canada, Justin Trudeau (who was a disaster, by the way), once said that living next to the United States was like "sleeping with an elephant. No matter how friendly and even-tempered is the beast," he said, "one is affected by every twitch and grunt." That's what Melania says, too. We have a border of sorts, in our bed. It's like a big wall of pillows and she tells me to "keep my trunk on my side," so that's a lot like what Justin's dad said. We are sleeping together and you're on top. Which is good, because my back is shot.

But I could still protect you. Your army is tiny, and you don't have guns. You need me.

Did you see how I dodged that bullet? Was that hot? I bet you liked that, didn't you? I was like Superman. It was, they say, probably God who saved me. That makes me the chosen one, like Anakin Skywalker in Star Wars or Keanu Reeves in The Matrix or Jesus in Mel Gibson's Passion of the Christ. They shot Jesus. They shot Kennedy. They shot Lincoln, Garfield and McKinley. They even shot Reagan and he survived but only I dodged a bullet. Because I was chosen by God. God wanted my presidency to happen the same he way he wants a volcano, a hurricane or a flood to happen. It's God's will.

Wouldn't you like me to protect you, Canada? I can protect you not only from the rest of the world but also from myself. I already do. And it's not cheap, the protection money. We are losing $200 billion a year on Canada. But I love you, so I'll protect you even more. I am building a dome. A Golden Dome, I call it. Sort of like my head. It's an incredible dome. It's like the Iron Dome that protects Israel from rockets but better. I won't bore you with all the science, but rest assured it is a better dome because it is golden. I looked at a silver dome and I said, "It would be better as a golden dome," and the generals, they said, "You're right, sir," so now it's very good.

And I know what you are thinking, Canada. You're thinking, *But nobody wants to fire rockets at Canada. People like us. Why do we need a Golden Dome?* Canada, my darling, I just want you to be safe. You live in a rough neighbourhood. And yes, that is my fault, but that part doesn't matter. There are a lot of people who hate America right now and not all of them have great aim. What if the bad guys are firing rockets at America and one bounces off our Golden Dome and hits you by mistake? Nice country you have there. Shame if anything happened to it.

But I don't want to see you hurt. So, tell you what I'm going to do. They say it's going to cost me $175 billion to build a Golden Dome. And if you want to be protected by the dome, it's going to cost you $61 billion, to be exact. But if you marry me, Canada, you can get the Golden Dome for the low, low cost of zero dollars. That's zero dollars American. What's that in metric money? Like $2 million Canadian? It's a steal. And if you act now, I'll throw in a set of Trump kitchen knives and a Trump meme coin for free! That's free minus shipping and handling. Of course, once you're our 51st state you'll be part of America, so you'll also be paying the $175 billion that the rest of the states are chipping in, but other than that, it's incredibly free. Think of the Golden Dome as an engagement ring.

I plan on visiting your parents at Buckingham Palace soon to ask for your hand in marriage, and also the other parts. I have asked permission to marry from the parents of all three of my wives. I guess I'm old-fashioned that way. I know King Charles will say yes. We have a lot in common. We're both nepo babies who love gilded furniture and, famously, cheating on our wives. But, my darling, my patience wears thin. I've never had to chase a woman in my life. Even back before I was president, I could have anyone I wanted. Like I said to Billy Bush on *Access Hollywood*, "When you're a star, they let you do it. You can do anything." But you? You're different. You'd never let me grab you by the Regina. You're so darn independent. Let me take care of you. Don't you want to have a hockey team that could win the Cup again? Then say yes. Just don't say "oui." I don't like it when you speak French.

Be my fourth wife and 51st state. We can have the ceremony in Niagara Falls. Or maybe Mar-a-Lago? Most of your family will already be there. Florida is full of Canadians. It's like Quebec with guns. Or Alberta with French. I just want you to know that this is the last time I will ask. After all, what is a Trump if he does not have his dignity? So, for the last time, Canada, will you be my 51st state? I won't ask again.

With all my love,
Donald J. Trump

PS: Okay. I'll ask again. How about now?

PPS: Now?

PPPS: Main tenant? Am I saying that right? The French for "now"?

PPPPS: Have you thought any more about that whole Greenland throuple thing? I'm seeing her on Thursday.

The Monarchy

One of my earliest memories is of the Queen. Not, of course, the current Queen, Camilla. I'm of an age where even saying Queen Camilla feels treasonous. Like most Canadians, there will only ever be one Queen for me.

In 1978, the Queen visited my home province of Newfoundland. I was just four years old, but I remember it all very well. I'd stood by the side of the road, frantically waving a little Union Jack long before I'd ever held a Maple Leaf. We didn't get many celebrities visiting St. John's in those days, and the whole town seemed to be steeped in monarchy mania—as if the city itself were a big tea bag bathing in a Brown Betty teapot.

Newfoundlanders have always had a soft spot for the Queen. After all, we were a British colony that had joined Canada only twenty-nine years earlier. In fact, we were the first place in the world to put Elizabeth on a stamp.

In 1932, the Dominion of Newfoundland issued a six-cent stamp depicting a six-year-old Princess Elizabeth. Twenty years before she took the throne, she sat on the corner of Newfoundland envelopes—curly-haired, looking like a young Shirley Temple, clutching a teddy bear, surrounded by rose and thistle and the words "Newfoundland Postage, six cents, H.R.H. Princess Elizabeth."

When that stamp was created, she wasn't meant to be Queen. Her uncle, King Edward, would not abdicate for four more years. The girl on the stamp might have grown up to be anything: an equestrian, a dog breeder, a gardener—or any of the other interests robbed from her by a life of duty. One of those hobbies was stamp collecting, and had history gone just slightly differently, this six-cent stamp in Newfoundland would have been her only appearance on one. However, history can be cruel, and the back of her head would go on to be licked some 220 billion times.

We lived on the outskirts of town and rarely made the trip to the centre of the city. But this was a special occasion. Only three people ever made it onto the hallowed space of our fridge door: the Pope, Jesus and the Queen. It would not be until 1984 that the Pope would visit, and we are still waiting on Our Lord, so a royal visit in 1978 was the closest we could get to the Second Coming.

"MyGodMarkWeGottaGetGoingNowWeGottaGet-ThreeDifferentBusesToGetAllTheWayDownThere, ChristOnACracker!" My mother spoke the way many Newfoundlanders do—in a machine-gun brogue where consonants tripped over vowels and *h*'s were abandoned in 'aste. Her people were Irish, and she stood firmly against everything the monarchy stood for—that is, until there was a chance to lay eyes on 'er. Then, suddenly, my mother turned as full English as black pudding and eggs.

"ThereSheIsMark, luh! There'sTheQueen! Queen! Queen! Queen! Luh, Mark. TheQueen! Queen? Queen? C'mere-Queen! HereQueen!" My mother called for the Queen as if she were an errant housecat escaped into the yard right before a big snowstorm.

I took her in with my young eyes and I could not help but feel a wave of disappointment wash over me. This was not the little girl I knew from the stamps. This imposter wore a navy blue hat with an upturned brim and the type of plain blue-and-white dress that some of the ladies in the front pews would wear to mass. This was not the Queen from the playing cards. This was not the stuff of Disney cartoons. This was not Cleopatra. This was a mother.

Had I really taken three buses to see yet another mom? I was four years old. I could see a mom anywhere! But my mother's enthusiasm for the Queen was almost as strong as my love for her, so I pushed my pudgy, pale hand through the temporary fencing and waved my flag. Hail Britannia, whoever she was.

A dour-looking little man walked alongside her, a cross between a bodyguard and a butler. He was an aide-de-camp, tasked with accompanying her on the royal visit and pointing out things that might be of interest. "Your Majesty, this is a library to be named in your honour. Your Majesty, this is the mayor. Your Majesty, this is a Newfoundland housewife screeching at you like a foghorn on cocaine."

My mother was easily excited, and she reacted to even the slightest bit of pageantry as if she was a can of pop in a paint shaker. Within seconds she would explode, her excitement and joy spilling over and shooting in every direction. As the Queen drew closer, my mother grew louder, the royal equerry looked more concerned and my arm grew more tired as it flapped in unison with my flag. I was trying to will the monarch nearer, hoping that if I waved hard enough, she would be caught in the tornado of my flapping and be drawn to my mother like Dorothy to Oz.

But the Queen did not stop. She glided past, clutching her handbag as if she feared my mother might steal her gum, or rubies, or whatever it was she kept inside that thing.

My mother snapped a photo at the last moment and forevermore the image would stay, protected under a sheet of cellophane, in our family album: a dour man next to the

Queen of England, her head partially cut off as she turned away from Canada and back to her rightful place on the money, the stamp and the fridge.

Every now and then, Mom would flip to that page and say, "RememberThatMark? RememberTheTimeWeMet-TheQueen?"

How many Canadians have that same memory? That same photo? That same sense of pride in a moment that didn't quite happen—except in the smoothed-over memories of our mothers? At the time, I don't think I really knew all that much about Her Majesty—Betty Windsor, as I like to call her—other than that she was the lady on the money. Every nickel of my meagre allowance was emblazoned with her portrait: Queen Elizabeth II on one side and a beaver on the other. Heads England, tails Canada. Every dollar bill (yes, I'm pre-loonie) stuffed into a birthday card from a kind aunt carried her picture. It was almost as if she herself were a distant relative sending me a card on my birthday: "Dear Mark. Congratulations on reaching the age of five. One wishes you an annus terrificus. Love, Aunt Betty (ER)."

Of course, you don't get a card from the monarch when you turn five. For that honour, you must reach one hundred years of age. A long-standing tradition from the reign of King George V saw the monarch send a telegram to any subject who made it to the century mark. One such letter reached a centenarian the day after the Queen herself died.

The message to Gwendolyn Hoare of Essex, England, read, "I send my congratulations and best wishes to you on such a special occasion" and it was signed "Elizabeth R." Who knew the Queen was in Manitoba when she died?

It just goes to show: Queen Elizabeth II was working right up until her death at the age of ninety-six. If she had lived just four more years, she would have found herself in the awkward position of writing a letter to herself.

Perhaps that's why so many Canadians—monarchists or not—have such a soft spot for the lady. She always showed up. As I aged, so did she. After the stamp, she went from the young lady on the twenty-dollar bills of my youth to the middle-aged monarch mom on the new bills in the 1990s to the distinguished nan on the notes put out in 2004. On those she looks a little like an original twenty that made it through the wash in the pocket of your favourite pair of jeans: a little wrinkled, a bit faded, but still unmistakably Betty. A comforting constant in our lives.

She survived twelve Canadian prime ministers, from Louis St. Laurent to Justin Trudeau, and even outlived paper money! The latest bills, debuting in 2015, feature an even older Queen, a great-grandmother, and are Canada's first notes to be printed on a polymer plastic base. The second image of the Queen on the bill, a holographic one, is the first portrait on Canadian currency to show her in a tiara. I think she finally earned a little flair.

Queen Elizabeth II was the longest-reigning monarch in British history. For seventy years and 214 days, she sat on the throne. I guess if you must sit somewhere for that long, a throne is a pretty good place to plunk your rear end. But your bottom is not the end you need to worry about when you are a monarch. Ask King Charles I. Or France's King Louis XVI. They say, "Heavy is the head that wears the crown." Maybe the person who coined the phrase knew that because he'd had to carry the King's head away in a basket after it had been chopped off. That's one heck of a workplace hazard.

The monarchy has always been a contentious issue. A popular monarch will have people bowing in reverence; an unpopular one will have their subjects storming the castle. A recent Ipsos poll shows that support in Canada for severing ties with the British monarchy has fallen to 46 percent. That's the lowest since 2016. Which is good news for the Royals because that also means that support for severing heads is down, too. Of late, things are turning around and, while not as popular as it once was, the monarchy is making a bit of a comeback.

So why the sudden surge in popularity? It's not because we have a young, fresh, hot King who is a hip and spry seventy-six years young. (Although 59 percent of Canadians think that Chuck is doing a good job, that's down from Queen Elizabeth's approval rating of 84 percent.) Canadians, it seems, aren't loving the Royals because of ties to England. Sixty-six percent of Canucks say they approve of the monarchy because it helps differentiate us from the United States. It's less about loving King Charles—and more about hating Emperor Donald.

But still, many Canadians ask: Why do we need a monarchy? Surely, after more than 150 years, we can break away from the land across the pond and stand on our own two feet. To many, having a monarch seems backwards. Insulting, even. Norway, Denmark, Holland, Sweden, these are all constitutional monarchies. But take a step back for a moment and look at the alternatives. Other countries vote for their heads of state. Countries like, say, I don't know, America. Which of these nations seems more tyrannical these days?

A monarch is neither Republican nor Democrat, Liberal nor Conservative. Trump may feel that he *is* the country. That it belongs to him. That the future begins and ends with his own golden visage. But the King reminds us that there is more to this country than the term of a prime minister. Yes, we have had political dynasties in Canada. (The Queen herself had to deal with two Trudeaus, and Caroline Mulroney may one day find herself at her father's desk.) But we do not have the patriotic pomposity that comes with the White House. The monarch is a reminder that our system carries on without us, long after we are gone. Like Queen Elizabeth—from little girl on a stamp to granny on a hologram—some things outlive politicians or even political parties.

The Crown is like a physical embodiment of the flag. The Crown is granted the power to govern Canada but entrusts it to the prime minister. That power is not his or hers to wield. It's an honour lent by the Crown, on behalf of the people. The Crown is above politics. It rests above the head, above the fray and above the petty squabbles that divide us. In America, the buck stops with the president. I'm sure that many Americans have at times wished they had someone else above Donald Trump. Someone constant to remind them that this too shall pass.

Over time, we have developed our own culture. Our own anthem. Our own flag. In 1982, Trudeau the First, I mean Prime Minister Pierre Trudeau, patriated the Constitution, minimizing the Crown to the symbolic role it has today. Some wonder, what's the point of all this symbolism? Why do we need it?

When Donald Trump began to talk about annexing Canada, Canadians looked to the King for some sign of support—not unlike a schoolboy who, told by the playground bully that he will be beaten up after school, runs home to Dad. At first, the Royal's support was underwhelming. When one of his realms is threatened, you might imagine a king rushing in to protect his kingdom in a suit of armour. You'd picture him like a Shakespearean monarch, on horseback, charging with his lance pointed at the enemy. "Verily I say, yon orange misshapen creature that dost threaten annexation, ye shall feel the sharpened end of mine stinging blade, and suffer the arrows of England's Crown!"

King Charles is supposed to stay out of politics. He must never show preference for any political candidate or party. He must not risk an international incident by overstepping his role. So he is muzzled in many ways. But the King can hint at how he feels. He can send little signals of support that can show that he is very much aware of Donald Trump's threats to Canadian sovereignty. Royal watchers are very much like birdwatchers. They don't miss a thing. King Charles spread his wings as far as he could from within his cramped gilded cage.

When he visited a British aircraft carrier, the King wore Canadian medals. "How unusual," the royal watchers noted. "He should be wearing his British medals!" He gave visiting Canadian dignitaries a ceremonial sword that carried his insignia. The sword was anything but a random gift. "Look," the palace paparazzi commentated, "a sword! To defend Canada with!" The signals kept coming, like heart emojis to a lover's text thread. He sat in a Canadian chair during a Commonwealth service. At a tree planting ceremony, he chose a maple. He sent a message congratulating Canada on the sixtieth anniversary of its flag.

And then, in a move akin to sliding a chess piece across a board to win a game, he came to Canada's Senate to read the Carney government's Speech from the Throne. He received a standing ovation from the assembled leaders. He read a promise to "protect Canadians and their sovereign rights." He supported the country staying "strong and free," said he saw "the fundamental rights and freedoms" in our Charter and said the government would protect "democracy, pluralism, the rule of law, self-determination and freedom." He danced around a lot of things but the dance he was doing was so Canadian it may as well have been "The Log Driver's Waltz". But there was one person he didn't mention. Donald Trump. He didn't have to. That was the whole point.

King Charles had only been King for three years and he was already into his second prime minister. When I first laid eyes on a Royal, I was just four years old. But in 2022, I was asked to escort then-Prince Charles on a visit to Newfoundland and Labrador.

On this auspicious occasion, I was to take the Queen's son to a local brewery, where he would pour a pint. "Who should we get to take the future King to a bar?" the staff in the Prime Minister's Office must have asked themselves. "I know!" the chief of staff probably shouted, the answer coming to her in a flash. "Mark Critch is the greatest drunk in the land. Pick him!"

I'd been told that once the Prince was handed off to me, he would be all mine. No one would intervene and it would be up to me to keep everything on track. I was the modern equivalent of the dour man. I had to keep to a strict schedule, stop only at the points of interest I had been told to and speak only with the guests of honour that were on the itinerary. This was the Prince's last stop on a royal visit to Canada, and when it was over I was to put the Prince and the Duchess of Cornwall into their car so they could immediately head to the airport.

I am not a details guy. Sure, I could take a guy for a pint, but just one pint? I had never done that before. I shuffled my feet in the gravel of the parking lot. This was the most awkward blind date of my life. What the hell was I going to say to this guy? "Saw your mother shovel something when I was a baby." I was out of my league. A fish out of water. Cinderella at the ball. I had heard the song "Someday My Prince Will Come" but I never thought it would happen to me.

This time, I stood on the other side of the temporary fence, and several locals asked why I was on the fancy side. I couldn't help but wonder what my mom would think as I stood, in my best suit, waiting for the Prince of Wales on the wharf in the village of Quidi Vidi. She had passed a couple of years earlier, and it would be just a couple of months before Prince Charles's own mother would meet the same fate. "Critch," some folks called out. "What are you at over there? You gonna ambush him?"

On the TV show I co-host, *This Hour Has 22 Minutes*, I had made a living by surprising politicians with guerrilla-style comedic interviews. Even the Mounties who lined the perimeter seemed a bit skeptical that I could behave long enough to play tour guide to the future King.

"Mark!" I heard a woman's voice cry out. "C'mere!" I walked over to the fence to see that the voice belonged to an older woman that lived in the community. I had met her a few times over the years, but she wasn't someone I knew well. I knew her in the vague way that everyone knows each other back home. "Are you going to be with the Prince?" she asked in an I-already-know-the-answer-so-don't-lie-to-me way. I had been sworn to secrecy while I was being vetted. I hesitated, but the hesitation revealed more than I could ever hope to say. I was busted. "I knew it," she said. "You got a good suit on."

"Our secret," I said, knowing it would be anything but. In Newfoundland, gossip spreads with an infectious speed that the COVID virus could only dream of. Not that I cared. Soon, Prince Charles would be delivered to me, and I would answer his questions and point out the various points of interest. "Your Royal Highness," I'd wax, "this is a wharf. And this, Your Royal Highness, is a big rock. And that, Your Royal Highness, is a seagull."

"Mark!" the lady shouted over the barrier. "I wants to meet the Prince." For a second I thought, *Maybe we could switch places and she can show him around*, but then I thought the better of it. I had my marching orders. Nothing I could do.

"Not up to me," I said.

"But, Mark," she said, "I got him a gift." She held up a large portrait of his mother. Picture something between the size of what you would see hanging outside a government office and one that might hang from the rafters of a hockey rink. It had a smoky hue and some water damage, and was not what an art expert might call "palace ready."

"My house burned down and this was the only thing that survived the fire," she said. "I think he'd like it."

There certainly was some smoke damage. Had I been an *Antiques Roadshow* expert, this piece would certainly have passed the provenance check. "He can't take that," I told her. "What's he going to do with it?"

"He might like to hang it on his wall," she said. "It's a picture of his mother. He must love his mother."

"He lives in Buckingham Palace," I exclaimed. "They have pictures of the Queen there."

She put the portrait back down, looking downcast. "I been waiting three hours," she told me. Somehow, I had become the royal complaint desk. "And Mark," she said, "I'll have you know that I'm a breast cancer survivor."

And there it was. In for the kill. A royal trump card. My mother had fought her own battle with breast cancer. I sat with her while she was given the diagnosis and felt the ground spin underneath us. My mother would never wear a crown or appear on a stamp, but she had been the Queen of our little house. To paraphrase the song, "Long she reigned over us but God did not save her."

I realized then that I didn't so much feel a connection to Queen Elizabeth so much as I clung to the joy she instilled in my mother. And then I remembered my mom, in 1978, standing where this woman was standing now, desperate for some acknowledgment from the distant relative on the fridge. If my mother had been in my spot, she would have torn the barricade down and escorted this lady to the front like the Queen she, too, was. We all have our little kingdoms, reigned over by our own Queen of Hearts.

The woman stared me down, waiting for my next move. "I'll see what I can do," I told her. "There's a little gap in the barrier over here. Stand there and if I get a chance, I'll bring him over."

"I knew you would," she said, grinning from ear to ear.

"IF," I reiterated. "And it's a big if!"

"I know you will," she said, settling into her new spot alongside a near-life-size picture of Aunt Betty. Just what I needed. More pressure.

In the distance I could see the crowd begin to sway and push in one direction like a wave crashing on the rocks. The Royals had arrived and royal watchers rushed to follow them. But my new friend held her ground.

Within minutes I was standing face-to-face with the man himself. He looked just like you'd expect—like he'd fallen off a cookie tin.

"How do you do?" he asked, reaching for my hand.

"Your Royal Highness," I countered, taking a hand that had shaken more hands than anyone other than his mother.

"They tell me you have written two memoirs and you have a television show that is based on one of them."

I was shocked. He had been briefed on me. I was worried that we would have nothing to talk about and now we were chatting about one of my favourite subjects—me! Indeed, I had developed a show based on my first book, *Son of a Critch*, co-starring Malcolm McDowell of *A Clockwork Orange* fame. In it I play my father, and a young lad from Yorkshire, England, Benjamin Evan Ainsworth, plays me. "It must be remarkable," the future King continued, "to see an actor portray yourself on television."

"Well, if anyone would know what that's like, it'd be you," I told him. "After all, a kid played you on *The Crown*." I could almost see the words fall from my lips and drift across the stiff Newfoundland breeze and into those famous ears. Prince Charles looked at me quizzically, as if thinking, *Who would bring up* The Crown *with the guy who will one day wear the crown?* Standing there on the wharf, I felt like one of the many codfish landed there, flipping about, suffocating. I looked about for a lifeline and there she was, just where I'd left her.

"There's someone I'd like you to meet," I told him, guiding the Prince of Wales over to the break in the barrier.

"Prince! Oh, Prince," she said, grasping his hand as if she had found an old family friend, which in some ways she had. "My mother loved the Queen," she told him. She held up her prized possession, the portrait of his mother. The Prince took it in as though it was the first picture of its kind that he had ever laid eyes on. He smiled, thanked her and began to walk away. "Hang on, Prince," she said, tugging at his famously thick fingers one last time. "You got to promise me something before you go."

Prince Charles turned to me for a moment and we shared a look. I wasn't quite sure whose side I was on in this particular game of tug-of-war. If I were a tennis referee, I would have to go to deuce.

I shrugged as if to say, "Let's hear her out."

He paused, turning back.

"You only get one mother in this world," she told him, "and one day she'll be gone. Promise me something, Prince. Promise me that you'll kiss your mother on the head every day and say 'I love you, Mommy.'"

He turned back to me and chuckled, saying, "My word. Can you imagine?" Breaking free, he carried on, waving to the onlookers and, perhaps, wondering what could possibly follow chatting about *The Crown* and being asked to kiss his mommy.

I gave the lady a nod and said "Good job" before jogging ahead to catch up with my charge. I brought him to the brewery, introduced him to the owner, and the Prince of Wales met the Prince of Ales. He poured his pint and tasted it and dozens of British cameramen got the picture that would run in all the tabloid papers the next day.

On the way out, I saw my wife, Melissa, amongst the crowd. I had already strayed from protocol once and my time as a royal escort was almost done, so I figured, what the heck. "Sir, would you do me a favour?" I asked.

"Of course," came the somewhat befuddled answer.

"That's my wife over there," I said, pointing in her direction. "I'd love to introduce you, if you don't mind. Gotta stay in the good books."

"One must," he said, chuckling. He walked up to her and shook her hand. "How do you keep up with him?" he asked her. "Two books. A TV show. It's really quite something." He really laid it on thick for me. I liked my new drinking buddy. He was a great wingman.

"Thanks for big-upping me," I said as we headed to his waiting car.

He laughed again. "Must stay in the good books," he said with a wink. We said our goodbyes as he got back into the car and he asked me to send copies of my show and I promised to do so, knowing I never would. Somewhere there must be a mile-high pile of well-intentioned gifts, portraits of his mother that will never hang and DVDs of TV shows that will never be watched. I wasn't about to add to the mountain. I'd taken enough of his time.

I walked home, the day's events bouncing around in my head. I wondered if, one day, I'd be taking my grandkids to stare at King William or even King George the way my mother had taken me. Would there even still be a monarchy by then?

This was in May. By September, the queen was gone and my old drinking buddy Charlie had become king. I wonder if he ever regretted not kissing his mother on the head and saying, "I love you, Mommy." Thankfully, I have no regrets.

Travelling Behind Enemy Lines

When I was a kid, a tan was a sign of wealth. It meant that you could afford to travel far from the freezing doldrums of a Canadian winter to someplace warm and sunny. Usually, that was someplace American. Sure, those Canadians lucky enough to live in British Columbia could soak up the rays on Crescent Beach, but not me. Europe was closer to our East Coast home than Vancouver. Nobody I knew vacationed in Canada. When a country is as big as ours, it can seem too big to conquer. It almost seemed a waste to fly all that distance without even crossing a border. Why fly to B.C. when it's cheaper to fly to Florida? That's one of the great mistakes Canadians make. We don't travel within our country enough. People spend their whole lives without ever bothering to see the place where they live.

My family took this to the extreme and we didn't bother ever seeing anything. Natural curiosity was unnatural to my parents, and we spent our lives like goldfish, forever passing the same leafy plants as we made tiny circles in the safety of our bowl. To us, a trip to B.C. or Florida was as likely as a trip to the moon or time travel. We did without the luxuries we did not need, sunshine being one of them. What did we need sun for?

The sun was something rarely seen in my part of the country. Even in summer, the sky was quite often grey. On the few blue-sky days we did get, my neighbours would walk out of their homes and stare up at the orbiting ball of fire in the sky with a mix of fear and wonder, as if it was a flying saucer. Yes, a tan was nice, but you'd probably burn first, and then peel. Too much of that and you'd soon be dead of skin cancer. Best to put a hat on and go back inside. We were indoor cats.

I hated the outdoors in general. Almost all of my childhood memories are of being cold. Being a kid in Canadian winter is not all hockey games and toboggans. I was constantly damp. My nose was always running. By the time I got to school, I was usually soaked through to the bone, my toes misshapen and wrinkled like a cardboard box that had dried up after being left outside in the rain. And no matter how long I dried my boots by the classroom radiator, they somehow remained cold and damp when I left to go home at the end of the day.

My cheeks were often red, but never tanned. After each winter break, the kids of the doctors and lawyers would come sauntering back to school a golden colour I could only dream of achieving from jaundice. They would regale their friends with tales of Floridian beaches and trips to Walt Disney World. "Oh, Cinderella's castle isn't all that big," they'd say as they grazed on Lunchables not yet available in Canada. "We didn't stay at the resort because my grandparents have a time-share in Orlando. I was cold when I got off the plane because I was still wearing my Mickey Mouse shorts." How I envied them. Not just because they had seen the castle that I had only ever seen on *The Wonderful World of Disney*. Not because the closest thing to sand I had ever felt between my toes was kitty litter I accidentally stepped in. No, I envied the heat they had felt and the colours they had seen, which were unlike anything I had experienced in my black-and-white world of a childhood spent in what felt like an eternal Canadian winter. The only thing I hated more than the cold was the inevitable question.

"Where did you go?" the rich kid would eventually ask me.

"Go? I didn't go anywhere. I'm right here," I'd stumble, desperately trying to avoid giving an answer.

"No. I mean for vacation," they'd say, leaning in, already knowing the answer. "Where did your family take you on vacation?"

"Oh, you know, we didn't go anywhere this year," I'd sigh, as if we had grown tired of our constant trips to Paris and Italy. "We just decided to stay home this year. You know," I'd offer, trying to save face, "they say you can't get ketchup chips in America. Interesting, that." I'd point this out, waving my fingers, red from ketchup dust, looking like I worked in a potato chip mine. The rich kid would usually roll their eyes with disdain. "I don't like ketchup chips," they'd say, barely hiding their disgust for their sedentary classmate.

As a boy, I hated being asked where I had gone on vacation. Now, as an adult, I hate it even more. As I write this, a headline in *The Globe and Mail* reads, "Canadians Go Elbows Up on U.S. Travel." I am reading that headline in Los Angeles. I know this makes me a bad Canadian. Now that I can finally travel, travelling isn't cool.

When President Trump threatened to annex Canada, Canadians decided that not only did they not want to be a part of America, but they also didn't even want to set foot there. And that decision made a big impact. Before he stepped down, former Canadian Prime Minister Justin Trudeau urged Canadians not to travel to the U.S. And for once, Canadians listened to him. "Canadians are hurt," he said. "Canadians are angry. We're going to choose to not go on vacation in Florida or Old Orchard Beach or wherever." In the new Canada, a tan is treason.

Canadians make up roughly a quarter of all foreign travellers to America. The months following Trump's threats saw a 24 percent drop in air travel to the United States, and that's not just Air Canada's fault. Canadians are choosing not to fly all on their own. This was matched by a double-digit drop in road trips over the border. That means a huge drop in backseat driving so we might even see a drop in the divorce rate. Canadians are choosing to spend their hard-earned dollars elsewhere, and Americans are starting to miss the seventy-four cents American—give or take—they get out of each one. Last year we spent over $20 billion in the States. That's nearly double the amount that Americans spend on McDonald's in a year. If you've ever seen Donald Trump from behind as he swings a golf club, you'll know that's a lot of money.

Amid the fog of the trade war, I should be somewhere more noble, like the Canadian side of Niagara Falls, which, ironically, with its casinos and cheesy hotels, feels like it should be the American side. But no. A business trip, long on the books and that could not be changed, meant that I had to go behind enemy lines like a Canadian spy. A double-double agent. The spy who came in from the cold.

Flying to the United States made me feel like I was cheating on my spouse. I didn't want to tell anyone where I was going, but I had to ask a neighbour to check my front step for packages. "Going away for a while, are ya?" they asked. I nodded, not offering up any more information. I felt like I was a kid back in school being questioned about my vacation by that rich kid, but this time the tables had turned, and anything but a staycation meant an altercation. "Business or pleasure?" they asked. Again, I nodded, shifting from foot to foot, wondering if it might have been easier to just let the porch pirates have whatever it was from Amazon that I no longer remembered ordering anyway.

"Where exactly are you going?" the neighbour asked.

"About a week," I said, retreating to my house to cancel any orders that had not yet shipped. Shower curtain with pockets to store things like shampoo? Cancel. Steering wheel tray table? Cancel. Portable fan that plugs into your iPhone? Cancel. Wait. I might need that for my trip. No! What am I doing? Cancel.

There was no escape from the judgmental looks at the airport, though. I sat in the lounge, hat pulled low over my eyes in case I might run into anyone. I looked around for any sign of a fellow traitor off to kiss the ring of Uncle Sam. I'm not sure what I was looking for. Mickey Mouse ears? A MAGA hat?

"Incognito, are ya?" a voice asked, jolting me the way a police siren would strike fear into the heart of a driver unsure if it was one or two glasses of wine they'd had at the neighbour's barbecue. "The disguise doesn't fool me. I know who ya are."

"Disguise? What disguise?" I asked.

"The big glasses and the hat. You're that comedian guy. No fooling me." A Canadian entertainer wearing a disguise to avoid being recognized is like Barron Trump wearing stilts to look tall. There are few things more anonymous than a Canadian entertainer. I wasn't wearing glasses to disguise myself. I was wearing glasses because I was nearsighted. And because I didn't want anyone to know that I was flying to the States, but you get the idea. Truth be told, I was kind of flattered that he might think me famous enough to have to bother.

"I watch all the Canadian stuff," he told me as he, very comfortably, moved my bag from its perch so he could sit in the seat alongside me. "*Schitt's Creek*, your show, the one with the guy who was in that other thing. I don't know your name, but I know the face." Ah. He was a real connoisseur. He did look the part of the proud Canuck. He wore a Roots T-shirt, the kind with their beaver logo on it, and sported a Toronto Maple Leafs ball cap that signalled he had the kind of loyalty that would never see him shirk his duties in hard times. "I'm off to Mexico. First time ever. Me and the wife usually go to Florida to watch the Blue Jays spring training, but not this time. No, sir. We're headed to Cancún. Ever been?"

For a moment I thought about lying and saying that I, too, was headed to Mexico, but I knew this would mean he might offer to accompany me to the gate and I'd be busted. "No. Never have," I offered meekly, fully aware that the inevitable was coming as surely as Canadian winter.

"I get ya," he noodled frantically. "It's dangerous. I hear they keep kidnapping Canadians, but they tell me the place we are going is safe." The Canadian government had issued a travel advisory for Mexico a few years prior, but that situation had calmed down. I didn't think Mexicans were hiding behind palm trees with big nets hoping a Canadian tourist might walk past and notice a doughnut on the sidewalk. Besides, something told me the only Mexicans this guy would see on his trip would be the ones serving his drinks. "Sure, it's dangerous, but I'd rather risk that than fly to Orlando this year. Elbows up, right?" He jerked his elbows up like an arthritic bird taking flight, and I couldn't help but notice his eczema. I was about to suggest he get some sunscreen on that before he flew away but he didn't give me any openings. "Hey," he said, interrupting himself. "Let me ask you something—"

Here it comes, I thought. *I'm about to be exposed for what I am. A fake!* This man considered me a Canadian celebrity, and now I was about to let him down. Luckily, he didn't know my name and didn't seem curious enough to ask. I could picture him next to his wife as they narrowly avoided being kidnapped at a swim-up bar. "You know who's not a very good Canadian?" he'd say to her. "That guy from the thing. Not the thing we like. The other thing that's on after it." I braced myself for the tsunami of shame.

“What’s your drink?” he asked.

A reprieve! Another moment to savour before I had to confess that I was nothing more than a backwards Laura Secord, running towards the Americans. All he wanted to know was what my drink was. I tried to think of what the most Canadian drink was. Molson? Labatt? Gin and Canada Dry? Bagged milk?

“You want to know what mine is?” he asked before I could answer. “An old-fashioned. Thing is, I can’t have one anymore. Know why?” *Because you never close your mouth long enough to swallow*, I thought, but figured the Canadian thing to do would be to not interrupt. “Bourbon,” he said, answering his own question. “I can’t drink bourbon anymore.” He stopped speaking. He looked at me with a knowing smile and I could tell that I was supposed to say something, but for the life of me I couldn’t think what.

“Doesn’t agree with you?” I asked. He was mid-fifties and about the age when doctors start telling you all the things you can’t have anymore to prolong your life, like liquor, and red meat, and fun.

“No,” he said, laughing me off. “It has bourbon in it. So now, I order mine with Canadian Club.”

“How is it?” I asked.

“Terrible.” He made the face you make when you accidentally taste a sour candy. It was the same face I was desperately trying not to make the longer we chatted. “I hate it, but that's all I drink now. Canadian Club old-fashioneds."

I didn't want the conversation to continue but I was fascinated by this man drinking Canadian Club old-fashioneds like a masochistic Opus Dei member whipping himself to prove his devotion. "Doesn't drinking something you hate kind of ruin your night, though?"

"It makes a statement," he told me with a fervour usually reserved for the pulpit. "It lets people know that I only buy Canadian."

"In Mexico," I clarified.

"Exactly," he said.

"You ever think of vacationing somewhere in Canada?" I asked.

He looked at me as if I had slapped him. It's one thing to drink a bad old-fashioned. It's another to try to find a swim-up bar in Moose Jaw. I could tell that he was beginning to think that I was questioning his loyalty. "Safe flight," he said, getting up and rejoining his wife across the lounge. I could see him gesturing towards me every now and then. He was probably telling her what a jerk the guy from "the thing" was. Confident in my obscurity, I headed to my gate.

Later, I stood there with the rest of my zone, watching the other traitors file onto the plane that would deliver us into the forbidden land. Their eyes were downcast and shifty, just like mine. I was one of them but couldn't help feeling a little judgy. I *had* to go, but them? They were likely going for some fun in the sun. I was working. Earning money that would be taxed. To pay for hospitals. I was practically saving lives! I could hold my head up high. And just as I did, my eyes made contact with the man from the lounge. He looked at me and then at my gate. Los Angeles. He shook his head and raised his smartphone. Click. He snapped a picture of me looking shamefaced in line for a flight to Los Angeles. He would surely text the picture to his friends.

"Look who I saw sneaking over the border," he'd smugly type into their group thread.

"Who's that?" someone would ask.

"That guy."

"What guy?"

"The guy from the thing."

"I don't know who that is. Should I?"

"Should you? Aren't you Canadian?" he'd type, maybe with a Canadian flag emoji for effect, so he could feel doubly superior.

Once we landed and I stepped outside of the terminal, the California heat reminded me that I was not where I was supposed to be. I felt slightly confused and out of place, like a bird blown off course. "Birdwatchers Startled to See White-Breasted Canadian Seabird So Far South," a headline would read next to a picture of me in shorts, easy prey for a bald eagle. I climbed into an Uber, finally feeling safe from Canadian eyes.

"Where you flying in from?" my driver asked. His accent and the flag tucked into his car visor told me he was Mexican American. I wondered if, had he not left home, he would have been impressed by my countryman when he demanded Niagara wine in his sangria. I settled in for my third grilling of the day, counting customs. "Canada," I told him, hoping he would show the general distance most Americans seemed to feel towards us.

"Oh! You're a goose! Or a duck or something, right?" I knew where this was going, but I put a confused look on my face and feigned ignorance. "Like a bird. You know? That's what they call it when you come down from the cold and the snow. Penguins. No. Come on, man, you know! What kind of a bird are you?"

I was not having much luck leaving my worries about my Canadian identity behind. "A snowbird?" I offered.

"Yes! Snowbird," he agreed enthusiastically. "You come down to get out of the cold."

I told him that I was not a snowbird. Technically, I explained, snowbirds are retirees who spend the colder months in warmer climates. I was not retired. I was on a business trip! Not pleasure. Business!

I wished that Americans would be forced to know as much about us as we did them. Back in my Canadian childhood, some of the commercials would be educational and feature short films that were humblebrags about Canadian heritage. The National Film Board even ran animated commercial-length shorts about our history. *Cool*, I'd think, my eyes inches from the TV screen, *a cartoon!* Next thing I knew I'd be tricked into learning about the Yukon or Confederation.

One was an animated feature that told the tale of the first train robber to use the phrase "Hands up!" Bill Miner was his name. His other claim to fame was that in 1906 he robbed the wrong train car and, instead of money, all he could find was a shipment of liver pills. Every Canadian over fifty who grew up without cable knows the final line: "The police found a gun and a bottle of liver pills. 'Hands up,' says the sergeant. 'Haaaands up.'" We were so desperate for our own stories to compete with the overwhelming torrent of American shows that even the humble story of Bill Miner became a story worth telling over and over again, wedged between ads for Kraft peanut butter and Hostess potato chips.

But my favourites were *Hinterland Who's Who*, short public service announcements that introduced viewers to Canadian wildlife. The beaver, the moose, the caribou, the loon. These slow-moving, softly narrated clips, scored by a haunting flute melody, were like Zoloft for eighties kids. Nothing stilled the excitement of watching Saturday morning cartoons more quickly. You'd be an inch away from the TV with radiation burns on your face, hopped up on sugary cereal, watching He-Man battle Skeletor, when all of a sudden they'd cut to commercial. Next thing you knew, you'd hear a narrator with a voice so soft he could calm a storm saying, "The loon is also called the great northern diver because of its ability to swim long distances underwater." You'd wake up an hour later, your head in your bowl and your face covered in milk, wondering what the hell happened.

I wish I had one now to educate this man on what a snowbird really was. It would star an old guy in a Hawaiian shirt driving along a beach in a Rascal scooter. "Each year, the Canadian snowbird migrates south to avoid the harsh Canadian winter," the narrator would tell us as the driver's eyelids grew heavy. "However, this year, many Canadians have refused to spread their tiny wings and fly away due to climate change. Once flying in the tens of thousands, the Canadian snowbird is now an endangered species. The weakened loonie means it is now harder than ever for them to find their preferred diet of cheeseburgers and Caesars. The only thing the Canadian snowbird hates more than Canadian winter is its apex southern predator, the orange-billed booby-headed dumb tit. For more information on the Canadian snowbird, check your parents' Facebook page."

"You will like living here," he told me, ignoring my protestations. "Much warmer than Canada. We get a lot of you." I told him he wouldn't anymore. I asked if he had noticed a decrease in Canadians coming down now that we were embroiled in a trade war. "What trade war?" he asked. He hadn't heard anything about the only thing Canadians were talking about. He hadn't even heard that Trump had threatened to make us the 51st state. Although he thought it would be a good idea. "Then you snowbirds wouldn't even have to leave Canada to be in America. You'd save a lot of money." For a moment, I started to explain that being American wasn't really the point, but thought better of it. He seemed blissfully unaware of us, and maybe the fewer Americans with Canada on their mind, the better.

But some Americans cared. I flicked on the news in my hotel room and saw a short story about home. I perked up the way Canadians do whenever American media bothers to mention us. A group of eastern American governors were meeting with their Canadian counterparts to plead for Canadian tourists to come back to the States.

The governor of Massachusetts was saying that tourism for her state and others such as Maine, New York and Vermont was down as much as 60 percent. And here I was, watching American TV in a thin Marriott robe that felt like a towel with sleeves. The only comfort I had was that the premiers were meeting with the governors in Boston. Surely, if they could have a cheat day, so could I!

Things had gotten so bad that the Maine Department of Transportation installed eleven signs throughout border towns to welcome Canadian visitors for the tourism season. I was impressed. They even had signs in both French and English. I thought that was a classy touch. A big sign on the side of the road that says "Welcome" is one thing, but a sign that says "Bienvenue" just seems so romantic. A lover must be wooed, after all. Then the reporter continued. "The signs will cost between forty-five and sixty dollars each," she said. Big spender. I suppose the sixty-dollar signs are the French ones? Even if they spent the full sixty-buck wad on all eleven of the signs, that would be a paltry $660. That's flowers-from-a-gas-station level of wooing. In 2024, Maine saw 797,900 visitors from Canada. They contributed roughly a billion dollars to the Maine economy. I wondered how much eleven signs for our side of the border that read "Frig off" and "Au revoir" would cost. In that moment, I was so angry I vowed never to go to Maine, from my hotel bed in Los Angeles.

On the way back, I stood in yet another line, this time at customs. For some reason, I always get nervous at the border. I'm as boring as can be, but I can't help acting as if I have a pound of heroin hiding in a body cavity. I fidget. I stutter. I sweat. I act guilty even though I don't have so much as a bottle of duty-free liquor on me. This time, it was even worse. This time, I actually was guilty of something. Being a traitor. Is this how Judas felt after the Last Supper? How many Tums did he need after dinner that night?

"How long were you out of the country?" the agent asked.

"Too long, am I right?" I had decided to double down on my love of Canada in case he was on the fence about letting me back in. He stared at me with the cold confidence that only those who have the power to order a cavity search own. "Two days," I said, abandoning my plan.

"Reason for travel?"

"Business." I said this with a shrug and an eye roll to show just how much I hated leaving home. But gotta pay the bills, right?

"Anything to declare?"

Yes, I thought. *I would like to declare that even though it wasn't technically wrong to visit the States, it felt like it was. I've never been ashamed to be Canadian but I feel, for the first time, ashamed to not have been a good enough one. Others have been holding fast, and it's making a difference. Hotels in Maine and distilleries in Kentucky are hurting just as much as Canadian businesses that have been hit with 25 percent tariffs, and that's not just because of prime ministers or premiers, that's because of hardworking everyday folks and, yes, even snowbirds. So I declare not to return to the United States, no matter what, until we break the bastards! I declare that I have been a cowardly traitor, but I won't do it again.*

"Anything to declare?" the agent repeated.

"No," I said.

"Welcome home," he said, handing me back my passport, something envied around the world.

I did not get a tan. And it felt great.

I'm Leaving You

Canadians are a family. The outside world, or our "neighbourhood," likes to think of Canada as the polite folks that never cause any trouble. We are the Ned Flanders to America's Homer Simpson. Other nations like to look at us as the picture-perfect family on the block. The nice folks at the top of the cul-de-sac who never turn up their music too loud and whose door is always open. "Why can't you be more like the Canadian kids?" they ask their states and counties. "They're always so well behaved." If they only knew. We never reveal our true selves to the world. After all, "cul-de-sac" is just a polite French way of saying "dead end."

Yes, Canada is one big family, but families fight. And if those other nations could look beyond our perfectly manicured lawn and neatly painted house, if they could peek behind our curtains when the northern lights were on, they might be surprised. Let's say they popped by around suppertime. They'd see all the provinces and territories gathered around the table and the sound they would hear wouldn't be laughter or polite conversation. It wouldn't even be chewing. The sound they would hear would be bickering. Loud, insulting, cutting, bilingual bickering.

Now don't get me wrong. Most of the provinces would get along. They'd even contribute to the meal. Every dinner would be a potluck. It would have to be because they wouldn't ever be able to agree on a menu. And so each family member would put their best foot forward and lovingly place their dish on the table as they jealously judged the other guests' contributions.

There'd be some Manitoban perogies and New Brunswick oysters as appetizers. There'd be Newfoundland cod with P.E.I. potatoes cut into Quebec poutine on the side. And if you are a fish lover, there'd be Arctic char from Nunavut and muktuk from the Northwest Territories. The second Ontario saw the northern spread is likely when it would remind everyone that a whale is not a fish and say that we should start the meal with a land acknowledgment in the same breath as they criticize traditional Inuit cuisine. The Yukon would argue that sourdough pancakes are not just for breakfast. Nova

Scotia would ask why no one had touched their donairs and then ask who drank all their Alexander Keith's beer without asking. And of course for dessert there'd be British Columbian Nanaimo bars, Saskatchewan berry pie and Ontario butter tarts. The table would be full and bountiful, and there would be more than enough for everyone. That table would be the envy of every other table in the neighbourhood.

But, sadly, we never see our families with the admiring eye others do, so, as there often is when people have nothing real to complain about, there would be complaints. After all, every family has some picky eaters. For instance, British Columbia would probably be vegan, and they wouldn't be able to stand the sight of the bloody Alberta steak on their plate. And, of course, Alberta wouldn't want to eat their veggies. So they would trade. And that's when the trouble would start. Alberta would ask Quebec to pass them the steak from B.C.'s plate in return for their veggies. Quebec would do what Quebec does and refuse to help unless they get to keep half of the steak and Alberta's dessert.

"What? Why?" Alberta would protest. "You've got your own steak!"

"Oui," Quebec would counter. "But I want yours."

"That's not fair!" Alberta would holler, upset because they had already been reprimanded for wearing their cowboy hat at the table. "There's nothing wrong with the steak on your plate."

"Non," Quebec would answer. "But someone else's just tastes better."

"I'll get it myself," Quebec would say, reaching for B.C.'s plate. "Pardonnez mon reach there, buddy."

"Arrêtez!" Quebec would say, pushing Alberta's hand away. "Nothing can pass through my place at the table. It is rude to reach over me. I am insulted. Now I want the whole steak." Quebec would take the plate from B.C.'s hand and begin to gnaw on a piece of their steak. "Little tough."

"Can I at least have my veggies back?" B.C. would ask.

"En français," Quebec would answer, their mouth full.

"Hey," Newfoundland and Labrador would say from across the room. "I was charging my phone over here and someone unplugged mine and plugged theirs in. Now my phone is dead."

"That is my phone. Don't touch it," Quebec would answer, scraping the contents of B.C.'s plate onto their own. "My phone was on 50 percent."

"So?" Newfoundland and Labrador would fume. "I was on 12 percent and it's my charger."

All the kids would complain. "Why does Quebec get to have seconds? And why is Quebec allowed to steal my power?" they'd shout as Quebec smiled the kind of self-satisfied smile that only the French can ever truly master.

"Leave them alone," Mom and Dad would say. "Quebec is . . . distinct."

I grew up hearing this a lot. When I was a kid, Quebec sovereignty was all over the news. In 1987, I was in the seventh grade. As I sat in French class, I began to wonder if there was any point in learning how to conjugate anything at all because it seemed like Quebec was always on the verge of leaving. What, I wondered, was the point of learning another language if the people we were learning it for were planning on separating? Who would we talk to?

I sympathized with them. I had a brother and I, too, often fought for attention. Every kid threatens to run away from time to time. I did when I was about ten. I can't even remember the reason now. Maybe it was because I wasn't allowed to stay up to watch a movie on television. Perhaps I was not allowed to sleep over at a birthday party. Or maybe I was negotiating for a higher allowance and decided to go full labour union and walk away from the table. Whatever the reason, the perceived slight was so big, so shockingly insulting, that I decided to run away.

I remember standing in the doorway of my parents' bedroom and announcing my decision. "Mom?" I said as she lay back on her bed flipping through a *Chatelaine* magazine. This was the golden hour of Mom's day. In between clearing up dinner and getting everyone ready for bed, she had a few moments of leisure at the end of the day when she could finally be alone with her thoughts. It was a brief respite when the needy parasites who sucked her soul dry all day were distracted by the television.

"Mom!"

She bent down the corner of a page and peered wearily over the cover. She said nothing, but waited, terrified but also curious about whatever fresh hell was about to pour over her.

"I'm running away," I told her. Even then, I had a flair for the dramatic and I delivered the line with all the panache one might expect from the third lead in a dinner theatre.

She snapped the magazine back to attention and spoke from behind its protective screen. "Oh?" she said, without any of the worry or alarm I had been expecting. "Sorry to see you go." If her voice could have been read on a heart rate monitor, she would have been pronounced dead on arrival. I couldn't get a read on her emotions at all because her face was fully obscured by a close-up of the 1980s model Monika Schnarre surrounded by hype lines that read "Is Your Marriage in Trouble?," "How the Royals Keep Fit" and "Child Care: Your Job or His?" In this house, it was most certainly hers, but she was shirking her duties. "You'll need a suitcase," she said.

This could not be happening. I was charming. Adorable. Young and helpless! I still had my baby fat and was working on my prepubescent fat.

"You can borrow mine," she said. "It's in the closet."

Fine, I thought. *I'll call her bluff.* I took the suitcase to my room and filled it up with all the things a ten-year-old imagines they might need in the outside world. Comic books, jeans, a picture book on World War II, gum, a sweater and an extra pair of jeans. If the world was run by ten-year-olds, the sock and underwear factories would surely go out of business. I closed it up and made my way back to my parents' room. By now, I expected my mother would be on her hands and knees, begging me not to take her precious baby from her. Surprisingly, she was still in bed. She was halfway through the magazine now and she had folded it in two. I could see her face, but her eyes and lips were still obscured by a recipe and an article titled "Spice Up Your Cooking: The Sexy New Ethnic Cuisine."

"I'm leaving," I told her, sounding like a fifty-five-year-old insurance broker who woke up one day and realized he was over halfway through his life and had never learned how to ride a motorcycle. "Goodbye, Mom. I'll call when I'm settled."

"Do you have any money?" she asked, turning the page to "10 Tory Promises to Women. *Chatelaine* Rates the PM."

I did not. To be honest, I thought I would have been stopped by now. My plan did have a few holes.

"There's ten dollars in my purse and some change in the ashtray. Keep the quarters for the phone." This was all getting too real. *She can't be serious*, I thought. *She must be bluffing*. Well, if she could bluff, so could I. I scooped up the change and took the money from her purse. A moment ago I had felt like an adult, but now, as I put the money in my pocket, I started to feel the tears well in my eyes. I rushed from the room, not so much for effect but to keep her from seeing me cry. I opened the screen door and walked down the front steps of our house. I was a hobo. A tramp. Nothing left now but to get a can of beans and a harmonica and ride the rails.

I walked to the end of our driveway, stopping occasionally to look over my shoulder. Surely the door would swing open and she'd come racing to my rescue? Nope. I checked the windows for the flutter of a curtain. Some sign that I was being watched, observed, minded. No such sign came. We lived on the edge of town in a house that faced a four-lane highway. I wouldn't dare try to cross it. Transport trucks and weary commuters whizzed by at sixty miles an hour. Wherever I was going, it was to the right. I quickly whipped my head around to look behind me one last time. No curtains swayed. No doors opened. I looked back to the road, and I weighed my options.

There was no turning back now. I stuck my thumb out and started to hitchhike. I prayed to heaven that no one would stop. But prayers usually go unanswered and a big semi geared down and stopped. The driver was no doubt shocked to see a ten-year-old hauling some Samsonite down the side of the Trans-Canada Highway. This was not a place where traffic ever stopped and soon the other cars and trucks were swerving to avoid us and honking at the unexpected obstacle. I froze for a moment, at a crossroads. On TV people hitchhiked all the time. David Banner would thumb a ride to escape the authorities at the end of each episode of *The Incredible Hulk*. And Richard Kimble would do the same in his endless pursuit of the one-armed man at the end of each episode of *The Fugitive*. But it was another of my favourite shows that came to mind then. *Unsolved Mysteries*. I turned and ran back up towards the house, tears streaming from my face. By now, my mother was halfway down the driveway to save me from whatever dangers awaited in the passenger seat of the tractor trailer.

This is what I thought of whenever Quebec separatism came up. Yes, Quebecers were going to say they wanted to separate, but did they really? Or did they just want some attention, like I had? Didn't they just want Mother Canada to come running down the road to tell them how distinct they were and give them ice cream? Being "distinct" was a big part of the separatist movement when I was a kid. I always thought that word a bit silly. Does that mean the other provinces are somehow "indistinct"? Are they blurry on the map?

In 1990, when I was in the tenth grade, the first ministers met to discuss the Meech Lake Accord. This was a set of constitutional amendments agreed upon by the federal and provincial governments in 1987. One of these provisions was to recognize Quebec as a distinct society within Canada and acknowledge that Quebec's French speakers were a fundamental characteristic of Canada. But when the time came to seal the deal, Newfoundland's new premier, Clyde Wells, refused to sign on, saying that the distinct society clause would grant Quebec special legislative status and undermine the Charter of Rights and Freedoms. Soon he was joined by the premiers of Manitoba and New Brunswick. Even former Prime Minister Pierre Elliott Trudeau stuck his nose in, saying the distinct society clause would undermine national unity. Then Prime Minister Brian Mulroney warned that if they didn't sign, Quebec's separatist movement could gain strength and tear the country apart. But Premier Wells called his bluff and stood his ground and the whole thing fell apart.

Disillusioned with a Canada that didn't see them as special, a coalition of Quebec MPs broke away from the major parties to form the Bloc Québécois. Its purpose? To promote Quebec sovereignty and, well, tear the country apart from the inside. Only Canada would have that. It's like buying bullets for your murderer. But it would be impolite not to, I suppose. And so, every vote in the House of Commons would forevermore go down as follows:

Liberals: Yes.

Conservatives: No.

NDP: Yes, but a little more yes.

Bloc Québécois: Whatever is best for Quebec.

And then, in 1995, things came to a head with the Quebec referendum. This was a vote to ask Quebecers whether Quebec should proclaim sovereignty and become an independent country. The ballot question was "Do you agree that Quebec should become sovereign after having made a formal offer to Canada for a new economic and political partnership within the scope of the bill respecting the future of Quebec and of the agreement signed on June 12, 1995?" The question was no clearer in the original French.

Quebec was getting ready to run away. Unlike my mom, who just sat there reading her magazine, Canadians from all over the country did their best to show them that they didn't need to go. In some ways, the whole mess had been started by Clyde Wells. And now another Newfoundlander (and future premier himself), Brian Tobin, then federal fisheries minister, would try to come to the rescue. He implored Canadians from outside of Quebec and around the world to come to Montreal to hold a rally for the "no" side. Airlines held a 90 percent off unity sale. Bus companies volunteered vehicles. The rally at Place du Canada had an estimated crowd of 125,000. I remember a planeload of people from my province going. It was filled with activists and entertainers carrying signs that told Quebecers just how loved they were. How special. How distinct.

Personally, I can't think of anything Quebecers would hate more than 125,000 Anglos descending on their town to ask "Où est la salle de bain?" in terrible accents. But somehow, the mood began to sway. When it was all said and done, the "no" side won with 50.58 percent of the vote. The country survived to fight amongst itself another day. Not that things ever really changed all that much. Even today, the Bloc Québécois leader, Yves-François Blanchet, is making his case against Canada.

"We are, whether we like it or not, part of an artificial country with very little meaning, called Canada," he said recently. I disagree. But, artificial or not, he lives in a country where he is allowed say that, *and* he gets a pension to say it. I think that sounds like a pretty great place. Yes, Canada is a family. And as any parent knows, the second you get one kid settled in for the night, the other will usually start crying.

And such is the case with Alberta. Canada's richest province can also, at times, be Canada's bitchiest. It wasn't long after the 2025 federal election that Alberta Premier Danielle Smith passed legislation that lowered the threshold for Alberta to hold a referendum on separation. No one was as upset about that as much as Quebecers. Bloc leader Blanchet said that if Alberta wanted to separate, it had to first define itself as, you guessed it, distinct. "I am not certain that oil and gas qualifies to define a culture," he said. Well, well, well, look who is a Canadian all of a sudden.

The Alberta Prosperity Project (APP), one of the groups driving a petition to force a referendum, says that Alberta is, indeed, distinct. They say they are against bilingualism and also "the Federal Government's support of wokeness, cancel culture, critical race theory, the rewriting of history, and the tearing down of historical monuments." So, yes, they want a culture that is distinct from the Canadian one. They want to be America. Their referendum question is much simpler than the one posed in Quebec in the 1990s; "Do you agree that the province of Alberta shall become a sovereign country and cease to be a province of Canada?"

I wonder how long before we see attacks from the Albertan Liberation Army. If there was ever a civil war in Canada, they would be the ones to watch. They have plenty of oil for their tanks, lots of ammo, and most of the people in the province are already wearing camouflage.

Jeffrey Rath, a rancher from Calgary who is one of the co-founders of the APP, seems to think that Alberta sovereignty means joining the United States. He travelled to the States with a "fact finding" delegation to make a case. Sadly, the Trump White House isn't the place you should think of going if you are hoping to find any facts. He said, "We have a lot more culturally in common with our neighbours to the south in Montana and with our cousins in Texas than we do anywhere else." The oil is always darker on the other side.

It seems that Alberta and Quebec are not happy in their relationship. Maybe it's time for them to go to couples therapy. I can see them in the therapist's office now, hugging opposite ends of the couch. Alberta on one side, in its finest western shirt, largest belt buckle and a ten-gallon hat (or, should I say, a 37.854-litre hat). Quebec on the other side, in a tight-fitting dress and heels, chain-smoking despite the lack of an ashtray anywhere in the room.

"What seems to be the problem?" the therapist would ask.

"She doesn't know the value of a dollar," Alberta would complain. "She's always turning up the heat!"

"So?" Quebec would fume. "I deserve to be warm! I get cold!"

"Then put on more clothes!" Alberta would shout, already losing it.

"I can't! I'm French," she would argue. "I am distinct."

"I'm sensing some tension between you," the therapist would say, intervening before things got out of hand. "I take it you're not getting along. Are you living together?"

"We've decided to separate," Alberta would say, waving Quebec's second-hand du Maurier smoke from his eyes. "We tried to stay together for our kid but—"

"Your kid?" the therapist would ask, thumbing through their notes.

"New Brunswick," Quebec would explain, lighting another smoke off of the inhaled butt of the last. "Half French. Half cochon."

"Hey," Alberta would protest. "No French in here. I don't understand it."

"You'd think he'd learn my language," Quebec would complain. "We've only been together for over 150 years. That's it! I want to separate!"

"Oh no you don't. *I* want to separate!! All she does is spend!"

"It's called equalization!" Quebec would roar. "It's in the Constitution. It's our pre-nup!"

"I gave her $13 billion because she said she needed it, and it turns out she posted a $4.8 billion surplus! She's been lying to me!"

"He's been seeing other countries!" Quebec would allege as she stormed around the room. "He spends all his time talking to America! I've seen the texts! My God, the spelling! He's cheating on me!"

"Oh yeah?" Alberta would say, pointing an accusatory finger her way. "You've been screwing Ottawa for years!"

"Ottawa pays attention to me! Ottawa thinks I'm special. Ottawa keeps me in the style to which I have become accustomed."

"Ottawa's a have-not province!" Alberta would shout, throwing his hat across the room. "That's my money he's been spending on you!"

"Okay, let's get back to the two of you," the therapist would say, trying to settle things down. "What about intimacy? How's your sex life?" The two provinces would grow quiet and awkward at the mention of such a deeply personal subject. "Alberta?" the therapist would ask in a calm and soothing voice. "Would you like to start?"

Alberta would cast his gaze to the floor, unaccustomed to being so vulnerable. "She won't let me lay any pipe," he would say.

Quebec would roll her eyes, having heard this all too many times before. "That's all he ever thinks about," she would mutter. "His pipeline."

"You know what?" Alberta would say, crossing the room to retrieve his hat from the floor. "To hell with this. I'm separating. And the quicker I do, the better. I'll finally be rich again."

"Oh, please," Quebec would growl. "You're not broke. You're cheap. If you just implemented a 5 percent sales tax you would make another $5 billion a year!"

"Oh, that's your answer? You're telling me that I should just go tax myself?"

"Well, you might as well," Quebec would say, strutting to the door. "Because you won't be laying any pipe around here tonight." Slam!

The therapist would make a short note in their notebook: *Irreconcilable differences.*

Quebec wants out. Alberta wants out. Maybe the only way forward is everyone gets out. Quebec can separate. Alberta can become its own country. British Columbia would call for "autonomous dependence," changing their name to BC/AD. The Atlantic provinces can form the new nation of Atlantis. The remaining western provinces could form the flattest country on earth, Maniwan. Nunavut, Yukon and the Northwest Territories would join forces as the Northwest East Territory, and for a while there'd be peace. Until Alberta realized they had no way to get all that oil to market so they'd merge with Maniwan. And Quebec, realizing that they needed the hydro energy in Labrador to keep the lights on, would offer to join Atlantis. Atlantis would accept, as long as they didn't start any of that "distinct" crap again. Ontario, initially shocked to learn that there were other parts of the country, would realize that building cars is all well and good but there's not much demand for cars when you can drive across your country in a day. And so, they'd rather sheepishly reach out to the other nations to see if anyone wanted a new province or state or whatever. Soon all the little countries would realize that maybe they would be better off if they formed one big country, and the confederation debate would begin. But hopefully, it won't get to that point.

When President Trump started slapping tariffs on Canadian businesses and talking openly about annexation, Canadians began to talk less of separation and more of unity. They've even come together to work on reducing interprovincial trade barriers. They signed agreements to boost the flow of goods, services, investments and workers.

They collaborated on ensuring products and credentials approved in one province are recognized in the others. They began to work on standardized health and safety regulations.

Prime Minister Carney introduced Bill C-5 to speed nation-building projects through the regulatory process. The One Canadian Economy Act aims to strengthen our autonomy and make us less reliant on America and more dependent on each other. And for once, the provinces and territories seem to be getting along.

They say that there will only ever be peace on Earth if we are invaded by aliens. The people of Earth would be so shocked and fearful of the little green men that they would begin to see the many different colours of people on Earth as brothers and sisters. They would become united by a common enemy. This seems to have happened to us in Canada. We have been warring with each other over our tiny differences for so long that we seem to have forgotten how very much we have in common.

After all this talk of separation, all it took for Canadians to become united was an invasion by a small orange man.

I Want My Flag Back

Canadians have never really wrapped themselves in the flag the way Americans do. Maybe that's because stripes are more slimming than maple leaves. We are the only country in the world with a leaf as a symbol. Something that will slowly wither and fall all on its own. We are "the true north strong and free" until, say, October. The American anthem refers to "the rocket's red glare" and "the bombs bursting in air," which "gave proof through the night that our flag was still there." Our anthem doesn't even mention our flag. Maybe that's because we couldn't handle a rake, let alone bombs and rockets. *O Canada, we stand on guard for thee*. Unless it's windy.

There is something beautiful about the fact that we are secure enough in our nationhood to make something so fragile our symbol. But why a maple leaf? Why not something more fitting, like, say, a cannabis leaf? With pot being legal, the plant we're best known for now is a weed. You wouldn't even have to fold the flag—you could just roll it.

The maple leaf has been a part of our identity since long before we decided to put it on our flag in 1965. The Société Saint-Jean-Baptiste, which celebrated French language and culture, adopted the maple leaf as an emblem in 1834. In 1836, the newspaper *Le Canadien* put a wreath of maple leaves on its front page. The editor wrote that the maple leaf had been "adopted as the emblem of Lower Canada." In 1850, Canadian pennies started to feature maple leaves. And then in 1867, almost a hundred years before it ended up on our flag, Canadian poet Alexander Muir composed the patriotic song "The Maple Leaf Forever" to commemorate Confederation. He was the principal of a public school in Toronto, and he was trying, without luck, to compose an entry for a national patriotic poetry contest when a maple leaf fell from a nearby tree and became stuck on his sleeve. Despite his best efforts to brush it off, it remained. So "The Maple Leaf Forever" is not so much a song about the eternal endurance of Canada. It's more about static cling. It's the Canadian version of Newton being hit on the head by an apple and discovering gravity, or Peter Parker being bitten by a radioactive spider and becoming Spider-Man.

For decades it was the unofficial anthem. It boasted that the "the thistle, shamrock, rose entwine / The Maple Leaf forever." The thistle for Scotland, the shamrock for Ireland and the rose for England. The maple leaf, however, for Canada. Those people in the 1860s sure loved gardening.

The Maple Leaf, our emblem dear,
The Maple Leaf forever!
God save our King and heaven bless
The Maple Leaf forever.

The song never really went away. In 1997, Anne Murray sang "The Maple Leaf Forever" before the final game played by the Toronto Maple Leafs at Maple Leaf Gardens. That's a lot of leaves. And Michael Bublé sang it at the closing ceremonies of the 2010 Olympic Games in Vancouver. Today, a silver maple tree at the corner of Laing Street and Memory Lane in Toronto boasts a plaque, erected in 1930, in honour of Alexander Muir, "who was inspired to write Canada's national song 'The Maple Leaf Forever' by the falling leaves of this sturdy maple tree." As it turns out, the sturdy tree was felled during a storm in 2013 and the pieces were used to make everything from nesting bowls for the Royal Ontario Museum to pens for soldiers serving overseas, lecterns for the Library of Parliament, a lap desk for the Speaker of the House of Commons, a bench in honour of late NDP leader Jack Layton and even a guitar played by Canadian folk rockers Blue Rodeo. Not bad for a tree that inspired a song that was never the official anthem. Still, maybe it's for the best that we don't stand every time "The Maple Leaf Forever" is played. With its pride in colonial plants and mention of the monarchy and even heaven, it might not have stood the test of time.

Of course, "O Canada" is not without its problems these days. Jamaican Canadian singer Jully Black swapped just one word in the anthem's lyrics and caused a stir in 2023. It was at the NBA All-Star Game when Black sparked debate by singing "our home *on* native land" instead of the familiar "our home *and* native land." This was not the first time, nor the last, that the lyrics have been revised. In 2018, the late MP Mauril Bélanger championed a change from "in all *thy sons* command" to "in all *of us* command." In February 2025, shortly after Trump announced his first round of tariffs on Canada, Canadian Grammy Award–winner Chantal Kreviazuk changed the lyrics during a 4 Nations Face-Off hockey game in which Canada played the United States to respond to comments about the 51st state. She sang "*that only* us command" instead of the official "*in all of* us command." How much longer before it's completely changed?

O Canada!
Our home on native land!
True patriot like that only us command.
With glowing hearts we see thee rise
(or sit if you're unable to stand),
The True North (though we recognize that there are
many other norths) strong and free!
From far and wide (and near and close),
O Canada, we stand (or sit) on guard for thee.

And this is where things get really tricky.

God (and by God, it could mean many different things
but be limited to the Christian belief, Yahweh, the God of the
Old Testament, the Great Spirit or Creator of many
Indigenous belief systems, or Muhammad, or for those
who do not believe in any one deity, maybe, just
believe in yourself, which we, as Canadians, are also
totally cool with) keep our land glorious and free!
O Canada, we stand (and sit) on guard for thee.

The maple leaf isn't even mentioned in our official anthem, but it did make its way onto our flag when we eventually got one. It's no wonder Canada did not win the space race. Neil Armstrong landed on the moon in 1969. We didn't get our own flag until 1965. We barely had something to plant on the surface! We have flown other flags in the past. Some flew the Union Jack. Many Canadians fought and died under the Canadian Red Ensign—the Union Jack with a shield emblazoned with Canada's coat of arms—during the two world wars. It wasn't until 1925, when Prime Minister Mackenzie King was in office, that Canadians started to get serious about having their own flag. He appointed a committee of public servants to investigate potential designs. But, being public servants, they didn't ever actually deliver the report. In 1958, a national poll of Canadians showed that 85.3 percent approved of having a national flag. Which makes you wonder what the rest of them wanted. Who doesn't want their country to have a flag? How Canadian. "Oh no. Don't want to be waving it in other countries' faces like that. Best to not draw attention to ourselves."

Prime Minister Lester B. Pearson raised the issue again in 1963. Think about that. The Beatles released "Please Please Me" before our country had a flag. The front-runner became sarcastically known as the "Pearson Pennant"—three conjoined red maple leaves on a white background with blue bars on either side. But because politicians can't agree on anything, a committee started to scour through five thousand submissions. A historian by the name of George Stanley came up with a single red leaf on white, flanked by two red bars. The committee's choice was unanimous. But when it reached the House of Commons, all hell broke loose.

Debate raged on for six weeks and 250 speeches. The *Toronto Star*'s Peter C. Newman called it "The Great Flag Farce." I can't imagine how things would have escalated if there had been social media in the 1960s. X would be on fire.

@Diefenbaker: Hey @PM_Pearson Nice Flag. LOL. It doesn't even need wind to blow. It does that all by itself.

@PM_Pearson: @Diefenbaker You'd know a lot about flags. I hear your mother was an expert when it came to poles. #MapleLeaf4Ever #Flag #Canada #DiefHatesTheLeaf

@Diefenbaker: Hey @PM_Pearson Your Maple Leaf is a big red flag. Canadians be warned. I hear they are made in China. Not very Canadian. Typical Liberal. Only the PCs will bring powerful flag paycheques home. #NotMyFlag #UnionJacked #DiefTheChief #HalfMast

@PM_Pearson: @Diefenbaker Gonna live to see your casket draped in that flag, Be-leaf me! #WaveGoodbye #Liberal #LeafMeAlone

Eventually, the flag was approved by a vote of 163 to 78. The royal proclamation was signed by Queen Elizabeth II on January 28, and our national flag was finally flown on February 15, 1965.

I assume it was because tensions were high on university campuses and Canadian students had nothing to burn in protest like their draft-dodging American cousins.

And that was the last time someone got really excited about the Canadian flag for a long time. Yes, it became a symbol of peacekeeping the world over. And yes, when obnoxious Americans travelled overseas, they would sew Canadian flags onto their backpacks to gain respect from Europeans and surreptitiously give Canadians a bad name. As a nation, we smiled when we saw the flag on the Canadarm in space. We waved it proudly on Canada Day as it flapped in the breeze beneath the fireworks. And we maybe even shed a tear when Tessa Virtue and Scott Moir wrapped themselves in it after winning Olympic gold. I saw first-hand the price we pay for that flag when I performed for our troops in Kandahar, Afghanistan, in 2006. Meeting the women and men who put themselves in harm's way on behalf of our country gave me a whole new respect for the Maple Leaf that is hard to describe. Knowing that 158 Canadian Armed Forces members would not only fight with that flag on their shoulder, but might come home with it draped over their coffin, made me think of the flag in a whole new way.

Flags can mean different things to different people. During the Vietnam War, some peace activists even burned theirs. I've never seen anyone burn a Canadian flag. But for a brief time, it was kidnapped and turned into a red flag for some and a white flag for others. In January 2022, the country was in a different kind of battle, but it was very much a fight for our lives. COVID-19 had changed the world and we found ourselves in lockdown, learning to hate the people we loved most. It was a depressing time of endless Zoom calls, nose swabs, bubbles and needles. But the country came together and we did our best to distance because we were in it together and the best thing we could do for our neighbours was to go it alone.

But not everybody felt that way. A group of truckers travelled to Ottawa to protest the COVID vaccine mandates and restrictions. About 85 percent of Canadian truck drivers were vaccinated, but a small and loud minority decided to make their feelings known by having a sit-in, and by sit-in I mean they sat in their trucks. They didn't want much, just for the prime minister to step down and for an end to all vaccine mandates. They said they wanted "freedom," and so they called themselves the Freedom Convoy. I would say having the power to blockade Parliament Hill and honk their horns day and night for weeks on end, holding the capital city hostage, is the very definition of freedom.

Justin Trudeau was not at the rally. He was isolating after coming into close contact with someone who had COVID. Which isn't surprising, seeing as he had personally hugged almost everyone in the country, and often shirtless. Conservative leader Pierre Poilievre did make it. He even brought coffee and Timbits to the occupiers. In 2020, when Indigenous protestors blocked a CN railway to protest a pipeline in Wet'suwet'en First Nation territory, Pierre had stated that "these blockaders are taking away the freedom of other people to move their goods and themselves. That is wrong and the government has laws and tools in place to combat it." When the protestors were Indigenous people protesting a pipeline, Poilievre asked, "How dare they?" When they were mostly white people protesting science, he asked, "Plain or chocolate-glazed?"

The Conservatives rushed to support the 10 percent of Canadians who were unvaccinated, like kids standing by the side of the road, tugging the air and shouting "Toot! Toot!" at a passing semi truck. Like those Conservative politicians, I, too, stood with truckers. But I stood with the 85 percent of them who supported the mandates.

Alberta Conservative MP Michael Cooper also stood shoulder to shoulder with the Freedom Convoy. He told the TV cameras, "These people have come to Parliament Hill to do what they have a right to do, and that is peacefully assemble and express their concern," but just to the right of him, or rather the far right, a Canadian flag was waving. On closer inspection, you could see that the flag did not just have a maple leaf on it. It was also dotted with swastikas.

Yes, the Flu Trucks Klan had a right to protest. A right won by veterans. Veterans who are memorialized by the cenotaph of the National War Memorial, which some protestors used as a parking space. The people memorialized by the statue also knew a thing or two about freedom and even Nazis. They knew about the common good. Which is why we wore masks and got vaccinated. To protect others.

Protestors also decided to give a statue of Terry Fox a makeover, tying a Canadian flag around his neck and covering him in a ball cap and pro-trucker signs. You may recall that Terry once led a convoy of sorts. Thousands of Canadians followed him on his Marathon of Hope. Hundreds of thousands still do today. His convoy was pro-science. If Terry Fox had been alive during that protest, he would have been an immunocompromised cancer patient whose treatment would have been delayed because hospital beds were filled with the unvaccinated. I wonder what side of the debate he would have fallen on.

Everywhere you looked, you saw the Canadian flag. And if you didn't see a Canadian flag, you saw a "F*ck Trudeau" flag. Those flags were used by the Freedom Convoy to show their displeasure with the prime minister in a subtle single entendre. Basically, if *The Dukes of Hazzard* was set in Calgary, the Duke boys would have had a "F*ck Trudeau" flag on top of the General Lee instead of the Confederate flag.

The "Free to be Dumb" Convoy loved flags. They wore them as capes, attached them to trucks. And at a certain point, something shifted. I had been proud of my country and proud of my flag, but I wasn't used to seeing it displayed as outerwear. I'd had shirts and hats with the flag on them, but I'd never seen it worn on its own like a towel. Soon, it was everywhere the anti-vaxxers were, and it had spread like COVID. It was hanging from trucks, cars, doors, anything but a flagpole. When I was a kid, having a flag in your window just meant that you were a university student and too poor to buy curtains. Now I didn't know what it meant.

The Canadian flag always seemed to belong to everyone and no one at the same time. It was the symbol of many different people, a mosaic of separate cultures, brought together as one family. A country with universal health care that knew that the good of the whole outweighed the needs of the individual. But now it felt like it belonged to someone else. Like it was a symbol of one group I had nothing in common with. Canadians looked out for each other. The mandates were for the common good, to keep our families, friends and people we would never even know safe. But now it belonged to one group. To one way of thinking. To one occupation. Whenever I saw one, I could almost hear them. HONK! HONK! HOOOONK!

It got to the point that if I saw someone waving a flag or flying it from their car, I'd feel myself seize up. My sphincter would tighten. I would back away and assume that the person flying the flag was going to be someone I would not want to talk to, or at the very least would give me COVID. Some new folks moved into an apartment around the corner from me. They flung a Maple Leaf over the rail of their patio. What did it mean? Were they hosers? Just regular Canucks who wanted to crush a few cold ones and listen to some Tragically Hip tunes? Or were they going to shout across the fence to ask if I was one of those suckers who got a booster shot? I felt as though the flag wasn't mine anymore. It had been co-opted by a loud minority who had changed its meaning. They hijacked it. They were hiding behind the flag, and I felt myself hiding from it.

I wanted my flag back.

Then the country began to heal. Not just from the virus, but from the wounds and scars left behind, the origins of which were harder to trace. The people protesting COVID restrictions found themselves without the cause that had become their whole personality. They could walk into any Walmart they wanted and cough on anyone they pleased. But somehow, the romance had been lost. And so, they wrapped themselves in the "F*ck Trudeau" flag full-time.

But then he stepped down before they could vote him out and they were left feeling empty inside. Somewhere in Canada there is a warehouse that is now overstocked. Half of it is filled with hundreds of thousands of N95 masks and the other half is stuffed with folded "F*ck Trudeau" flags as far as the eye can see. That day is done.

In 2025, as Canadians found their patriotism rejuvenated, I began to see the Maple Leaf more and more—flown not out of hate but out of pride. This time, it didn't hang from trucks. It wasn't being worn as a cape. It was being given the respect it deserved. I went to my summer place. In Ontario, they'd call it a cottage. In Newfoundland, we call it a cabin. Either way, it's home. I opened a Canadian Tire bag and took out the brand-new flag I had purchased on the drive out. I rolled the sleeve onto the little pole that stuck out of the side of my house. I stood back and watched it flapping in the breeze. I felt a weight lift. I finally had my flag back.

And may those ties of love be ours
Which discord cannot sever,
And flourish green o'er freedom's home
The Maple Leaf forever!

CanCon Artist

I am a CanCon kid. I grew up in the 1970s and '80s. This was a golden age of Canadian content. It was a time when *SCTV* was just as important as *SNL*. Music videos by Canada's Glass Tiger were just as talked about on the playground as videos by Bon Jovi. I was weaned on Canadian television. I'd much rather have Mr. Dressup as a neighbour than Mr. Rogers. And *Sesame Street*'s Mr. Snuffleupagus was great, but *Polka Dot Door*'s Polkaroo was my preferred plushy puppet that only some people could see. For me, Canadian artists were just as much a part of pop culture as the American or British ones. That's not because their art was necessarily better than the others'. It was all thanks to the least artistic thing of all—government interference.

The Canadian Radio-television and Telecommunications Commission rules over the Broadcasting Act of Canada. The CRTC is like a police force for TV and radio. Much like a restaurant can't open until the health inspector checks for rats, you can't get on the airwaves until you have been tested for your Canadianness. Before you could have a prime-time show in this country, you would have to do a sort of drug test. You'd have to pee in a cup, and if there was enough maple syrup in your bloodstream, you'd be given your licence. There's a ten-point system for key creative roles (writer, executive producer, director, etc.). Six out of ten must be Canadian if you are to get the CanCon stamp. Getting it means you're able to access much-needed funding and get your art on a broadcaster where it can be seen by Canadians and, hopefully, the world.

Some folks will say, "If your art was any good, you wouldn't need CanCon regulations." The people who say that are usually the ones who can't get the CanCon stamp. It's complicated. Take *The Handmaid's Tale*, written by internationally bestselling and multiple-award-winning novelist Margaret Atwood. Her novel, which prophetically chronicles the final year of the current Trump administration, was made into a hit series for a streamer. It's written by one of the all-time greatest Canadians. Canada features as the morally superior country that the characters fight feverishly to get to. It's filmed in Canada. But it does not count as CanCon. Why not? The star, screenwriters, network and primary setting are not Canadian. However, *The Tudors*, a historical drama about King Henry VIII and Anne Boleyn starring Irish actor Jonathan Rhys Meyers and filmed in Ireland, did count as CanCon. Why? I can only assume that a series about English royalty in the sixteenth century counts as a Canadian prequel.

Yes, the system is flawed, but I would argue that it is desperately needed. If CanCon has proven anything, it's that when Canadians are given the opportunity to hear Canadian voices, we will take them to heart. Those voices just need a little help getting heard. We have no choice but to listen to American content. We live next to a neighbour that is playing their music so loud that we can barely think. All CanCon regulations do is allow us to turn up our stereo loud enough that we can hear our own music over all that noise. I've always found it funny that in Canada we have a word for our own content and not one for the content from the States. That's because AmeriCon is everywhere. There's no escaping it.

AmeriCon is even on the Canadian networks. CTV and Global TV pepper Canadian productions alongside the American shows that they get to air. For every homegrown comedy hit like *Corner Gas*, or the Canadian family-friendly cop show *Hudson & Rex*, there are a dozen American sitcoms like *The Big Bang Theory* or American reality shows like *Survivor*. The Canadian shows, popular as they are, are the loss leaders. For those networks, selling ads on American shows is the business model, and making CanCon is the price of doing business. They buy Canadian rights to air the big American network shows like *Law & Order*. They don't have to make those shows or waste time hiring Canadian creatives or crews, so there's a lot more profit to be made. But if they actually want to put that profit in their pockets, then they must make some Canadian shows. It's a sort of creative tax. Only the CBC has a mandate to make exclusively Canadian content.

Now, with streaming and social media, it's harder than ever before to get Canadian content in front of Canadian eyeballs and ears. Gone are the days of the three-channel universe: CBC, CTV and static. Back then, my parents would plop me down in front of the TV set and switch on the only babysitter I ever knew. It was thick, heavy and solid. A television was a real piece of furniture back then. I'm sure there was more radiation bleeding from a single 1970s TV set than there is in most nuclear reactors these days. The TV set I grew up with needed some time to warm up. You'd turn it on and a tiny dot of light would flicker to life in the middle of the tube. The warmer it got, the closer you were to getting your fix. The anticipation was a part of the high. You'd pace. Tap the top of the set. Fiddle with the rabbit-ear antenna, hoping that it would have some effect. You'd check the screen with the back of your hand, the same way you'd check your forehead in the morning for signs of illness on a school day, hoping for some form of heat. You had to be careful, though. Eventually, the electric hum would get loud enough, and an image would fade into view. If you were supposed to be doing your homework and you swore to your parents that you hadn't been watching TV, all your mom had to do was touch the top of the TV with her hand to know you'd told a lie.

You'd take what you could get back then. You didn't care what country it originated from. It was television and you wanted it injected directly into your eyeballs. It could be anything, game shows, cartoons, daytime talk, cop shows—anything but soap operas. Come to think of it, there never were Canadian soap operas. Soaps, both daytime and nighttime versions, were huge in the 1980s, but we never produced one. *Dynasty* and *Dallas* were both nighttime dramas that followed feuding oil tycoons. But as far as I know there was never a version set in Alberta. I guess oilsands aren't as sexy as gushing geysers. Joan Collins and Linda Evans made TV history ripping their gowns and pushing each other into a pool as they fought over a man. I guess it wouldn't feel the same in a Canadian soap. Two housewives, one from Calgary, one from Edmonton, falling onto the ice and tearing their hockey sweaters as they argued over which team would win the Cup.

You couldn't have a Canadian version of a soap like *General Hospital*. Not with the Canadian healthcare system.

It's hard to be sexy when you're stuck on a stretcher in the hallway. A Canadian soap set in a hospital could only be called *Waiting Room*. People would meet, fall in love, marry, cheat on each other, divorce and start all over again before ever having seen the doctor.

BLAKE

Dammit, Chelsea. When I met you, I was just a carefree man with a shooting pain in my arm and a burning sensation in my chest. And you were just a girl with a dream. A dream of seeing someone who could tell if your knee was infected or not. Me, an unlucky fool who took a number and that number was 349. And when I met you, you were just a kid. A kid they called number 678. Well, that's my lucky number, see? Sure, there were other women. Number 252. But that's over now. She was broken but she's in a cast now and gone. But you and me? They say we're not really emergencies and we may never be seen, but I see you, Chelsea. And you see me. So, what do you say we try again? Push these two chairs together and make a roof out of these *Maclean's* magazines and make a home for ourselves. Right here. Right now.

NURSE

Number 678? Chelsea? Number 678?

CHELSEA

Goodbye, Blake.

BLAKE

Noooooo!

Come to think of it, I would watch that.

We may not have had Canadian soaps, but we had Canadian versions of everything else. The Canadian TV connoisseur would start their day with *Mr. Dressup*. This is, perhaps, the greatest Canadian show ever made. Ernie Coombs was born in America. He began his career as an assistant to the king of children's entertainment, Mr. Rogers. But Coombs was that rare thing, an American who moved to Canada in the 1960s and hadn't even been drafted into the Vietnam War. I loved Coombs's show *Mr. Dressup*. Not because it was educational, which it was. Not because of the puppets, which it had. No. I loved *Mr. Dressup* because it was *on*. I'm sure there was something else on. Maybe a daytime talk show or a preacher relieving people of their maladies and their pocketbooks. But *Mr. Dressup* is what was on in my living room.

The bar wasn't too high for daytime television back then. Less so for children's television and even less so for

Canadian children's television. The premise of *Mr. Dressup* was simple: A single, childless man would invite kids over to his house so they could watch him change his clothes. His friends included an alligator and a semi-conscious owl and a mute dog. The most popular character was a small child with an Australian accent and a bowl cut who lacked forearms or any control of his legs. Despite this, the boy lived, not in Mr. Dressup's house, but in a tree-house in the backyard. Now that I'm an adult, it seems like a house of horrors, but as a boy it was exactly where I wanted to be. The biggest lesson Mr. Dressup wanted to leave you with was to "keep your crayons sharp, your sticky tape untangled, and always put the tops back on your markers." But the greatest lesson he taught me was of patience, kindness and calmness.

The pace of Canadian children's television was akin to what you might experience in a sensory deprivation tank. It was nothing to spend ten minutes just watching Mr. Dressup slowly cut up an egg carton. It was like if cooking shows took the time to peel each individual potato. No. To grow them. A typical craft might go:

MR. DRESSUP

I think it would be nice to make a giraffe from cardboard. Let's go over to the crafting table and give it a

try. I'll just open the drawer here. That's good. Now, we should get some cardboard. Three pieces should do. And I'll get the sticky tape. And of course, our safety scissors. And some markers. One yellow marker. One brown marker. One black marker. Now, let's open the caps and test them. Yes. That's good. That one, too. And that one. Excellent. Best to get all these caps back on, now. We don't want the markers to dry out, of course. One. Two. Three. There we go. Now. Let's mark the different pieces of a giraffe. The long, long neck. The body. The four legs. The tail. Now to do that, of course, we are going to need to take the caps back off the markers . . .

And it wasn't just Mr. Dressup who somehow kept children's attention with banter the pace of which you could only find in a hospital elevator. *The Friendly Giant* was the Robin to Mr. Dressup's Batman. And the man who played him, Bob Homme, was another American expat. Oh, for the days when the only thing coming over the border were gentle children's TV show hosts with puppets.

That show featured a giant who lived in a castle with two friends, a red-and-blue giraffe named Jerome and a rooster that hung from a bag that was nailed to the wall. Children's television had a pattern: a host with a memorable characteristic (cross-dressing, gigantism), flanked by two unnerving puppets, one of whom lived someplace unsettling, be it a treehouse or a bag.

Each episode of *The Friendly Giant* started the same way. The camera would pan across a little village. You never saw any people. Had the giant eaten them all? Then you'd be ushered into a castle that looked like it had been constructed from toilet paper rolls and mud. The doors would open and the giant's hand, about the size of a dump truck if the scale was right, would rearrange some furniture. As he described it, "Here's one little chair for one of you and a bigger chair for two more to curl up in. For someone who likes to rock, a rocking chair in the middle. Now look up. Look way up." First you'd see a boot that had to be the size of the first storey of a house. Then you'd see the rest of him. A gentle, grey-haired giant with a bowl cut, not unlike that of Mr. Dressup's squatter, Casey. The CBC hair department must have saved a lot of money, as they seemed to be using the same safety scissors Mr. Dressup used on construction paper.

As a child I was fascinated by the scale of things. Rusty the rooster was about the same size as Friendly's hand, which meant that this bird was about the size of a garbage truck. Why did Friendly eat all the townspeople when he had enough chicken to run an abattoir for months? How did the rooster get in the bag on the wall? Was he a prisoner? Or had he chosen to live there? Why hadn't he taken a spot in the empty chairs below? Rusty also played the harp. I knew it was a puppet, but I just couldn't believe that a bird would have the wing dexterity to play an instrument as delicately plucked as the harp.

Jerome was a baritone-voiced giraffe who only ever poked his head in through a window. This also confused me. If the castle was big enough for a giant, why was the giraffe forced to stay outside? Maybe he was just smart and knew that if he dared enter the giant's castle, he, too, could end up nailed to the wall in a bag.

The giant played the recorder. This was the one instrument every Canadian child was forced to play in school. To this day, I can still smell the spit-filled thing and hear the asthmatic wheeze of thirty squeaking instruments blowing out "Three Blind Mice" and sounding like it was being played by nails on a chalkboard. This recorder must have been made from a redwood. Sometimes, they would be accompanied by three cats who played jazz. I bet that castle smelled a lot like weed.

Like on *Mr. Dressup*, not much ever happened on *The Friendly Giant*. There were no explosions or battles. No one was ever upset. The conversation never moved past pleasant chit-chat. It was the oatmeal equivalent of American

TV's sugary cereal. It was warm and filling and easy on the tummy. Each episode ended in the same way. Friendly would play "Early One Morning" on the recorder. He would put the furniture away and say, "It's late. This little chair will be waiting for one of you, and a rocking chair for another who likes to rock, and a big armchair for two more to curl up in when you come again to our castle."

I'd be sad to see them go, but I knew they'd be back again the next day. There was a quiet comfort to those CBC mornings. Yes, I could have watched American TV. But these shows felt like home. You got the sense that the people entertaining you may not have the biggest budgets or the flashiest sets, but they cared. Not just about their work, but about you.

We even had our own cartoons. They had a handmade feel that stood out from the slick American fare like *He-Man* and *G.I. Joe*. *Rocket Robin Hood* answered the unasked question: What if Robin and his merry men lived not in Sherwood Forest but in space? The animation wasn't overly animated, to say the least. It was more a series of drawings set to music. They reused the backgrounds over and over again. Even as a kid, I knew it was cheap. The same company made the first *Spider-Man* cartoons and Canadian talent voiced them. The company was so cheap that they recycled two whole episodes of *Rocket Robin Hood* as *Spider-Man* cartoons. They just replaced Robin with Spidey on the animation cells, changed the dialogue and they were done. We kids had been suspicious, but it was hard to prove. Back then, you couldn't just download the episode on your phone. You had to wait for reruns. And even then, to compare, you'd need a *Spider-Man* rerun to air sometime close to a *Rocket Robin Hood* rerun. We hadn't paid a dime to watch the shows, but we still knew we were being ripped off.

That was the thing about Canadian TV in those days. You could tell that it was Canadian. The lighting was a little washed out. The clothing a little faded. The stars not quite Hollywood glamorous but more like the-prettiest-person-who-worked-at-your-local-supermarket glamorous.

Even the game shows were a little sad. *Definition* was a bit of a *Wheel of Fortune* rip-off that aired on CTV. It was only missing the wheel and the fortune. The thing that *really* set Canadian game shows apart were the prizes. Most prizes were overstock from a retail warehouse, and contestants often wouldn't know what they'd won until after the show had been taped and they were back home. The prizes we'd see on TV were dubbed in after the fact. Could be a box of cake mix. Could be a home barber kit. A coffee maker. Or the grand prize—a microwave! On American game shows you could win a car. On Canadian game shows, you might win something that you had in your car.

Congratulations! You're our grand prize winner! You'll be heading home in style with a 1987 Chevrolet Caprice's winter tires. These are two beautiful winter tires that can fit a 1987 Chevrolet Caprice. If you have a 1987 Chevrolet Caprice, you'll love these 225/70 R15 tires with sport suspension. These will also fit an '87 Dodge Ram van or a Lincoln Town Car but they did come off a Chevrolet Caprice.

Bumper Stumpers, *Reach for the Top*, *Pitfall*. There were dozens of CanCon game shows that offered Canadians a combined tens of thousands of dollars' worth of prizes. One show, *Supermarket Sweep*, showed contestants racing through a supermarket to see who could grab the most valuable groceries within a time limit. The prize was literally a full cart of groceries. Producers would never be able to afford to make that show today.

"Congratulations! You managed to get four steaks, a bag of potatoes, some frozen pizzas, four litres of milk and some scallops. You've earned prizes totalling $300,000."

The longest-running Canadian game show of all time, *Front Page Challenge*, was also the longest-running Canadian show of any kind. It started in 1957 and ran for thirty-eight years. Growing up in the 1970s and '80s, living with parents who wanted to watch this show was the equivalent of having a power outage. You might as well not have the TV on. It was the driest show from an industry known for making shows that were drier than a mouthful of crackers in the desert. Each week, a panel of Canadian journalists would try to guess the identity of a mystery guest before the timer went off. The guest would have made the news recently, so the panel was guessing not only the identity but also the headline. Guests were flown in from all over Canada and the world. Martin Luther King Jr., Eleanor Roosevelt, Anne Murray, Indira Gandhi, Gordon Lightfoot, even Malcom X came to play. All very interesting, unless you were a kid forced to watch it. Of course, no kid was ever forced to watch *Front Page Challenge*. But no matter what was playing on the only TV in the house, if it was on, you were watching. And so I spent many years curled up on the floor in front of the TV watching someone guess the name of the latest Canadian newsmaker.

PIERRE BURTON

Is it a Canadian story?

MYSTERY GUEST

Yes.

PIERRE BURTON

Is it a national story?

MYSTERY GUEST

Yes.

PIERRE BURTON

Is it an English Canadian story?

MYSTERY GUEST

Yes.

PIERRE BURTON

Is it a political story?

MYSTERY GUEST

Yes.

And on and on it went. But in the three-CanCon-controlled-channels universe of my youth, this was must-see TV. As the years went on, and the cast grew much greyer and older, you got the impression that they wouldn't even be able to guess their own identities, let alone that of a mystery guest.

FRED DAVIS

Okay, panel. Your mystery guest is panellist Pierre Burton. Any guesses as to who he is?

PIERRE BURTON

Is he an entertainer?

FRED DAVIS

No.

PIERRE BURTON

Is he a singer?

FRED DAVIS

No. And let me remind you, panel, we already know that the mystery guest is not an entertainer.

PIERRE BURTON

Is he an actor?

FRED DAVIS

No. Any other panellists? Betty Kennedy?

BETTY KENNEDY

Is it me?

FRED DAVIS

No. But you're getting close.

BETTY KENNEDY

Is it a singer?

But we were not without our excitement. *The Beachcombers* was another CBC series with a homemade feel. It ran from 1972 to 1990. In those days, being a character in a television show was like being in the royal family, and the only way out was by dying. It followed the exploits of a group of guys in British Columbia who salvaged logs that had broken away from barges and logging booms. The hero, Nick Adonidas, piloted the true star of the show, his logging tug, *Persephone*. His rival, Relic, had a black speedboat that was guaranteed to jump a log at least once an episode. The Americans had *The Dukes of Hazzard* with its orange Dodge Charger. Canada had a logging tug. In the States, you had the bar on *Cheers* where everybody knew your name. In Canada, we had Molly's Reach, a café where Nick and Relic would threaten each other over pie. And everyone really did come together on *The Beachcombers*. The show was the first to incorporate Indigenous cast members and storylines. Nick's partner was Jesse, played by Pat John, a member of the shíshálh Nation. His sister was also a main character, and Chief Dan George, an Academy Award–nominated Canadian actor and chief of the Tsleil-Waututh Nation, was a regular guest star. *The Beachcombers* checked every CanCon box in the game. It was hyper-local. Super-regional. And very Canadian. Without it, an East Coast boy like me might never have known about the prevalence and danger of rampant log crime.

In 1988, after sixteen years' worth of stolen logs, the CBC decided it was time to give the aging show a new look. So they removed *The* from the title and retitled the show *Beachcombers*. This did not help much, and the show was cancelled in 1990. They tried to revive it in 2002 with a series called *The New Beachcombers*. That didn't help either. They brought back some of the cast from the original series, but most of the cast had since passed on, and log theft was no longer the most pressing criminal activity in British Columbia.

Crime was also the focus of one of CTV's most popular shows. The premise of *The Littlest Hobo* was: What if *Lassie* had a smaller budget? The show looked like it was shot on a microwave, but it was appointment television. Each week, the dog would wander into a new town. He had no owner, hence the eponymous "hobo." You don't hear that word very often anymore, but it was a simpler time. The dog would find some crime or wrongdoing, solve the case by pawing at a door or circling a well and, problem solved, he would wander off down the road again to the next person in need of help.

What set this dog show apart from all the others was the theme song. *Maybe tomorrow, I'll wanna settle down. Until tomorrow, I'll just keep moving on.* You could stop any party or hush any bar by singing the first couple of lines of that song. In fact, it probably stands up there with the best of Neil Young or Gordon Lightfoot when it comes to beloved Canadian folk songs. That's the power of CanCon. That's the power of a shared experience. That's the kind of thing that instantly makes a group of strangers feel like a family. Maybe that's the greatest case *The Littlest Hobo* ever solved. He wandered into Canada, united us with a catchy theme song and then wandered off to the next place.

CanCon gave us a fighting chance to have our own pop culture. These shows might not have been produced were it not for the CRTC. They may not have been as slick or flashy as their American counterparts, but they had heart. And they could not have been made in any other country. They were by us, for us and of us. Even when they were mocked, they had a way of coming back stronger.

One of the greatest and most successful Canadian exports was *SCTV*. John Candy, Eugene Levy, Martin Short, Catherine O'Hara, Dave Thomas, Rick Moranis, Andrea Martin and the list goes on and on. The show was innovative, hilarious and distinctly Canadian. But not even *SCTV* was Canadian enough for the CBC. To meet CanCon requirements, the network demanded two minutes of purely Canadian material in every episode. The cast couldn't believe it. The show was written and performed by Canadians. It was even filmed in Edmonton. Dave Thomas shot back, "What the hell do you want us to do? Sit in front of a map of Canada, put on toques, drink beer and eat back bacon?" And that's exactly what they did.

"Great White North" was a two-minute sketch in which Thomas and fellow cast member Rick Moranis played Bob and Doug McKenzie, two hoser brothers with a TV show. The characters became cultural icons in

Canada, spawning a hit movie and a top-selling album that peaked at number 8 on the American *Billboard* 200 album chart in 1982. A sketch meant to lampoon Canadian content regulations was a hit in the United States. Today, there's even a statue of Bob and Doug in Edmonton. "Take off, eh?"

These days, shows like CBC's *Schitt's Creek*, the brain-child of *SCTV* alum Eugene Levy and his son, Dan, prove that Canadian entertainment can compete on the world stage. That show went on to be the first show ever to sweep all the comedy categories at the Emmys.

Canadian content regulations lift our content up. When I flip through the channels of my mind, many of the shows that I think of are the result of CanCon: *King of Kensington*, *Wayne and Shuster*, *The Hilarious House of Frightenstein*, *Degrassi Junior High*, *Corner Gas*, *Due South*, *The Kids in the Hall*, *The Nature of Things* and on and on and on.

Lately, producers have been adapting American shows and slapping the word "Canada" onto the title. *Entertainment Tonight Canada*, *Big Brother Canada*, *The Amazing Race Canada*, *Family Feud Canada*, *The Price Is Right Canada*. How long before there's a *Miss America Canada*? Or *Good Morning America Canada*? I don't think this is what was intended. But in today's fractured world of streamers and social media, I guess you have to make a buck where you can.

The world has changed. The big streamers argue that they shouldn't be held to the same standard as traditional broadcasters. The CRTC wants them to invest 5 percent of their Canadian revenues into making more Canadian content under the new Online Streaming Act. Netflix, Disney+, Apple and others plan to battle the CRTC in court. For their part, the CRTC says they plan to modernize the definition of Canadian programs.

In the end, as we've seen in the past, it's not really up to the courts, the CRTC or the streamers to define what "Canadian" means. Nor is it in their power to tell us what to watch. Canadians will find the shows that speak to them. They'll quote them, like they do *Letterkenny* and *Trailer Park Boys*. They'll share clips from them to make them go viral, like they did with *Schitt's Creek* and *This Hour Has 22 Minutes*. They'll watch them, but not because they're some kind of pill they are supposed to swallow. They'll watch them because they can't get enough.

Operation Trojan Moose

Donald Trump isn't the first American president to underestimate Canadians. During the War of 1812, Thomas Jefferson said that invading Canada would be "a matter of marching." But when Canadians (technically the British, but we'll take the win) burned down his White House, it proved to be more of a matter of matches. Maybe it's time for Canadians to once again get fired up. I have a sneaking suspicion that Lady Liberty might even lend us her torch to do the job. But we should be careful. It would be a much more dangerous job these days. Donald Trump has blinged out the Oval Office with so many faux-gold trimmings and gaudy polyester fabrics that the blue flame might burn forevermore.

Jefferson wasn't the first president to covet his neighbour's country. Abraham Lincoln's secretary of state,

William Henry Seward, also wanted to move the property line and take our lawn. He had already bought Alaska and, like any good developer, wanted to expand after securing the corner lot. He proposed an invasion of Canada, but Lincoln figured he'd had enough trouble fighting other Americans in the Civil War.

Of course, we were British North America back then. Seward wanted Canada before even Canadians did. He wanted to make it American North America. He wanted to "Make America Great for the First Time." Maybe it didn't catch on because MAGFTFT doesn't look as good on a red hat. He believed in Manifest Destiny, that God himself wanted the U.S. to rule over North America. That's not quite what Trump believes. Seward believed it was God's will, while Trump believes he is God.

There is nothing new under the sun, or in our case in Canada, under the clouds. The States wanted to purchase Greenland in 1867, too. A report commissioned by Seward stated that if the U.S. owned Greenland, to the east of Canada, along with newly purchased Alaska to the west, Canada would want "peacefully and cheerfully, to become a part of the American Union." Canada would give up because it was surrounded. But what Seward saw as a big hug, Canadians viewed as a chokehold.

Seward was obsessed with Canada. His desire was almost sexual. He wrote passionately in his journal of the object of his affection, dreaming of Canada's "wheat-fields in the West, its broad ranges of chase at the North, its inexhaustible lumber lands, the most extensive now remaining on the globe, its invaluable fisheries and its yet undisturbed mines." It's almost as if his borders weren't the only thing expanding.

Seward and friends bought Alaska from the Russians for $7.2 million U.S., or roughly the price of a two-bedroom condo in Vancouver today. Just a few days later, Queen Victoria signed the British North America Act, creating the Dominion of Canada. But that did not include British Columbia or Rupert's Land. Rupert's Land was made up of what is now Manitoba, Saskatchewan, Ontario, Quebec, Alberta, Nunavut, the Northwest Territories and even Montana, Minnesota and North and South Dakota. That left a lot of meat on the bone. It's probably a good thing that Rupert's Land didn't last because it was owned by the Hudson's Bay Company. If it still existed today, it would be bankrupt. But back then, like with the HBC, people thought it was too big to fail.

Seward wanted to annex Rupert's Land and British Columbia to give Americans a straight run to Alaska. But the northern colonies, who had been fighting amongst themselves, realized that the only way to hold off the American invaders was to come together into a confederation. In just the same way, Canadian premiers have tried to come together to break down trade barriers under threat of Donald Trump's tariffs.

In 2025, Canadian patriotism is at an all-time high due to the hungry eyes of our neighbours. This is nothing new. It was Seward's expansionist rhetoric that spurred Canadians to unite the British North American territories and solidify our nationhood. We owe our very existence to American expansionism. The bigger the threat from America, the better Canada gets. And back in the mid-1800s there seemed to be another threat of American invasion every few years.

The year 1838 saw the Pork and Beans War. This war might just be the most Canadian conflict ever. It all started when New Brunswick lumberjacks fought with lumberjacks from Maine over which lumberjacks had the right to jack the lumber from which trees. The Pork and Beans War got its name because beans were the preferred meal for burly, bearded men in plaid on both sides of the border. So I guess you could say, the Pork and Beans War was the first war ever fought over gas. Soon, so much gas built up that militias from both countries mobilized on the border. The U.S. Congress sent a force of fifty thousand troops to relieve the pressure before something blew. There were no casualties. Lumberjacks from each side just stared at each other with their axes over one shoulder, breaking wind. Eventually, the U.S. gave more land to the U.K. and the U.S. government paid Maine and Massachusetts for their loss. Both countries would have peace and plenty of Christmas trees. And there would be no more pork-related wars until 1859.

That's right. The next skirmish between Canada and the U.S. was the Pig War of 1859. The killing of a Canadian pig drew together thousands of troops and several warships. This happened between Vancouver Island and the state of Washington. The pig had wandered into an American garden and started eating potatoes. The farmer, from Kentucky, did what men from Kentucky might do when confronted by a foreigner and shot it, to protect the lives of himself, his family and his potatoes. The pig's owner, who worked for the Hudson's Bay Company, was justifiably upset and demanded $100 in compensation. The American was willing to pay only $10. This was the first time in history that someone had called HBC out for their inflated prices. In his defence, the American said that he had no choice but to shoot the pig because the pig "was eating my potatoes." The Canadian replied, "It is up to you to keep your potatoes out of my pig." When authorities attempted to arrest him, his neighbours called in the army.

Soon, 461 Americans with fourteen cannons were squaring off against five Royal Navy warships mounting seventy guns and carrying 2,140 men. All over one pig and a couple of potatoes! Canada and the United States were going to war over what amounted to a barbecue. The commander of the Royal Navy refused to escalate things into firing bullets "over a squabble about a pig." In the end, the only living thing to die in the Pig War was the pig, and historians agree it was delicious.

Living next to the United States is a bit like hitting the pubs with a friend who can't handle their liquor. Everything is fine and dandy for the first while. You have a few drinks, maybe some wings or nachos, and you stroll down memory lane. Soon, a story about an ex or a perceived slight from years ago rears its head and the next thing you know their finger is inches away from your face and you're telling them to "calm down, buddy." America and Canada are great friends, until America remembers that we are there. Every few decades, without fail, they have a few drinks and they want to invade us. It's not their fault. America is a nice guy. They just can't handle their oil.

In 1930, the United States War Department asked the Joint Army and Navy Board to develop a secret plan to invade Canada. Code name: War Plan Red. It wasn't personal. They came up with plans to invade all of their friends. War Plan Brown was for Mexico. War Plan Yellow was for China. They even had War Plan White in case of a domestic insurgency. We don't know much about who came up with the plan names, but we do know that they were kinda racist.

War Plan Red wasn't even focused on us, really. It was developed in case of a war with Britain. Instead of directly attacking the U.K., the Yanks figured it best to invade Canada before the Brits could use their Commonwealth ally as a foothold for an invasion of America. They didn't even really want to invade us. How rude.

War Plan Red was well thought out. First, America would have to capture Halifax. They figured they would send twenty-five thousand troops by sea to take it. This seems about right, considering you would lose about five thousand straightaway to local pubs and about two thousand would immediately defect after meeting local gals. The port there was a strategic hot spot and, historically, an important base for British ships. They planned to use poison gas to take it. Clearly, no one planning this invasion had ever stood on top of Citadel Hill. You could drop all the poison gas you wanted to, but once the wind picked up, the only people dying would be in New Brunswick.

And if they didn't win? They would destroy it. "If Halifax could not be captured, its denial to RED as a base by means of air and naval operations, should be attempted." Can you imagine? After being destroyed by the Halifax Explosion in 1917 and then rebuilding, there was a plan to level it again by Americans in 1930. This was no Pig War. Next, they had to take control of the hydroelectric plants at Niagara Falls so they could control the power grid and leave Canadians in the dark. Then they would attack Montreal, Winnipeg, Toronto, Quebec City and Vancouver. This would upset the populations of St. John, Calgary, Hamilton, Nanaimo and Regina, who would ask, "What? So we're not good enough to invade?"

Charles Lindbergh, the aviation hero who made the first solo transatlantic flight, flew secret reconnaissance missions up to Hudson Bay to find weak spots in Canada's defences. In 1957, Jimmy Stewart, the beloved star of the Christmas classic *It's a Wonderful Life*, played Lindbergh in a movie about his life. Now, here was Lindbergh flying over Churchill, Manitoba, trying to figure out the best way to bomb it. It was Lindbergh who suggested using chemical weapons to take us out. He later turned out to be a Nazi sympathizer, so maybe that makes sense.

In 1935, the Americans spent $57 million to update the plan. The military even carried out the largest war games in U.S. history, using thirty-six thousand troops to practise less than fifty kilometres from the Canadian border. In 1935, they built three military airfields along the Canadian border. However, they said these were just civilian airports. When the cat got out of the bag, President Roosevelt had to release a statement saying that the Americans had no intentions of invading Canada. They may not have had intentions, but they did have a plan. When World War II broke out, all other plans came off the table and the Yanks focused on just one folder, War Plan Orange. Japan.

Still, I am shocked. How could our greatest ally be so underhanded, so dishonest, so two-faced as to develop a plan to invade us behind our back? Canadians would never do that, would we? Actually we did. And we did it first. On April 12, 1921, the Canadian military came up with a plan to invade the United States. We, however, didn't have the military expertise, the money or the number of troops that the Americans had. Perhaps, more importantly, we didn't have the marketing skills. The U.S. plan was called War Plan Red. The Canadian plan, the brainchild of the Canadian director of military operations and intelligence, Lt. Col. James "Buster" Sutherland Brown, was called Defence Scheme No. 1.

Let's take a closer look at that. First, "Defence"? I know that the best offence is a good defence, but that word doesn't exactly strike fear. And "Scheme?" A scheme is something that con artists whip up to trick you into buying black charcoal toothpaste or bitcoin. Canada had the "Mambo No. 5" of invasion plans. It was a one-hit blunder.

Let us not forget: the worry wasn't an American attack on Canada. This was meant to be the first punch thrown in a war between the U.S. and the British Empire. According to Buster's Defence Scheme No. 1, Canada would hit the U.S. as hard as it could, then wait for our big brother Britain to come and finish the job for us. When the time came, western Canadian troops would seize Portland, Seattle and Spokane. Vancouverites attacking Seattle is sort of like that episode of *Star Trek* where there are two Spocks that fight each other. Prairie Command would take Fargo and march on to invade Maine. And once Maine fell, the plan was to retreat to Canada and blow up bridges and railways to slow down the enemy. So Buster's big plan was to attack, run away and hide.

Buster took the whole thing terribly seriously. Unlike the Yanks, Buster didn't have any fancy Lindberghs. He did the reconnaissance himself. He put on a disguise—not that anyone in Fargo was likely to say, "Wait a minute! Isn't that Lt. Col. Buster Brown? We must be under attack! Run!"—then he drove down to New York and Vermont in his Model T, snapping photos on his Kodak camera on the way. It sounds to me like Defence Scheme No. 1 was more like Paid Vacation Scheme No. 1.

His writings show that he was not very impressed by what he saw. "If Americans are not actually lazy," he wrote, "they have a very deliberate way of working and apparently believe in frequent rests and gossip." He wrote this while stopping to gossip. He added, "The women of the rural districts appear to be a heavy and not very comely lot." Sounds like old Buster was turned down a time or two.

In 1928, Defence Scheme No. 1 was terminated by Chief of the General Staff Andrew McNaughton and many of the documents related to it were destroyed. But what if they hadn't done away with it? What if we'd reignited the flame that burned down the White House during the War of 1812? What if we had another Pig War in response to Trump's threats of annexation? This time, however, it would be because the Americans elected a pig. We'd call it Operation Rabid Beaver. We would attack by land, sea and, most terrifyingly of all, Air Canada. And, as we all know, nobody wants that.

First we would take Alaska, and they probably wouldn't even notice the difference. They're used to moose and flannel. Then the Pacific Command would move on to occupy Seattle and Portland. All we'd need is coffee, craft beer and the Fifteenth Division of the Pacific Command's Special Forces Unit, Arcade Fire. The band has dozens of members, and the hipsters of Portland and Seattle wouldn't be able to resist the pied piper–like allure of Arcade Fire's eclectic baroque pop art rock. Their vegan hearts would stop under the shock of the assault, combined with their already poor circulation from wearing skinny jeans.

Prairie Command would then annex North Dakota (or, as it would be renamed, Southern Manitoba). The Great Lakes Command would make an organized raid across the Ambassador Bridge. No longer would we argue over which side of the falls is prettier, because it would all be the Canadian side! Then Quebec Command (because you have to give them their own distinct fighting force) would trek through the Adirondacks, securing our position by turning all Trump Hotels into Fairmonts. To paraphrase the great

Leonard Cohen, "First we take Manhattan, then we make poutine."

The Maritime Offensive would reclaim Maine, which would become known as Newer Brunswick. Meanwhile, in the south, the Snowbirds would take Florida, led by Gen. Anne Murray.

Americans think Canadians can't invade them, but Justin Bieber is their children's idol, the two sexiest American men are Canadians named Ryan, Margaret Atwood is their favourite author and *Schitt's Creek* is their favourite TV show. We've already invaded their dumb country without firing a shot, and they didn't even realize it!

Or, if we really want to take over the United States, maybe we should just let them invade us. I'd call it Operation Trojan Moose. Consider the electoral implications of Canada joining America as the 51st state. Let's look at the House of Representatives. In the U.S., the allocation of House seats is based on representation by population. That's roughly one seat for every 761,169 people. Canada has about forty-one million Canucks, giving us 54 seats in the House and two senators. That's a big drop from Canada's current 343 seats in the House of Commons and our 105 senators. But if it were to give us a chance at undoing the United States, maybe we can do without P.E.I. having four seats and Mike Duffy as a senator.

And how would this work, exactly? Well, most Canadians would likely vote Democrat, especially after we were forced to join the United States. That would mean a Democratic House majority almost every time. Plus, we would most likely end up with two Democratic senators. It's not a huge number, but it might be just enough to mess with President Trump's next Supreme Court confirmation. And how fun would that be? But the *really* fun part would be the state of Canada's fifty-four Electoral College votes. If Canada's vote went blue, we might have enough power to keep the Republicans from ever getting into the White House again.

Donald Trump isn't the first president to underestimate Canadians. But if we play our cards right, he just might be the last.

Monuments

Americans love their political heroes. They do much more than put their faces on currency. They carve them into mountains. They build giant monuments and larger-than-life statues. They turn them into godlike immortals who can do no wrong.

A few years ago, I found myself in Washington, D.C., on a stroll along the National Mall. It's a landscaped park lined with iconic memorials to America's political heroes. Spend one day there and you'll quickly realize that they do everything bigger in the States. The Washington Monument is both a stunning memorial to their founding father and the gold standard of phallic symbols. Americans were never known for their subtlety and, boy, does it ever show there. That obelisk is anything but an oblique representation.

That's a hell of a thing for poor old Honest Abe to be staring at all day. The statue of Abraham Lincoln at the Lincoln Memorial, just a short walk away, truly is a wonder to behold. Chiselled from white marble, Lincoln is nineteen feet tall; he'd be twenty-eight if he was standing. If you include his pedestal, Lincoln's monument comes in at a towering thirty feet. In contrast, the Washington Monument is 555 feet tall, and George Washington didn't even have to get shot to earn it. Thomas Jefferson's memorial statue, on the south side of the Tidal Basin nearby, is also nineteen feet tall, but he doesn't even get a chair. Martin Luther King Jr.'s statue stands opposite Jefferson across the basin and is the tallest, at thirty feet. His is the first memorial not dedicated to a president, a white man or the thing white presidents often cause: wars.

Keep strolling and you'll see groups of veterans, some in uniform, some in anything but, but with one thing in common—a promise to never forget. They gather around other iconic memorials to the Second World War, the Vietnam War, the Korean War and on and on. There are so many memorials to wars that you'd think Americans might one day get the point and learn from them and stop embroiling themselves in so many wars.

If the United States were a house, the National Mall would be the mantel over the fireplace. The place where the family photos are kept so you can brag to the visitors. It's where they keep their most treasured mementoes. At eye level, where everyone can see. The memorials in the National Mall are there to create the mythology America wants the world to see and its own people to believe in. They help distract from the tragic loss of all the people shot and shift the focus to how heroic those shot must have been. America is the modern Rome, and Rome must have its gods.

There is no comparable space in Canada. The Speaker of the House of Commons, Francis Scarpaleggia, recently declared the United States to be "modern-day Rome in size and power." He then added, "We are Athens in culture, values and democracy. That is how we must see ourselves. That is who we must be." Prime Minister Carney agreed, stating, "We are Athens, and they are Rome. We will win. We are in the golden age of Athens."

Athens has the Parthenon, the Zappeion, the Erechtheion. They had temples to Athena Nike and Olympian Zeus. The Athens analogy refers to democracy, public discourse and education. But surely, if we are to be the new Athens, we should have a couple of statues? I have spent a lot of years wandering around our nation's capital. As a correspondent for CBC's *This Hour Has 22 Minutes*, I've had the good fortune to see more of the Parliament Buildings than most Canadians have. I've been in the prime minister's office several times. I've swung from the flagpole atop the Peace Tower. And I even once brought NDP leader Tom Mulcair to the Centennial

Flame, where we roasted hot dogs on sticks to celebrate his retirement. I've admired the Parliament Buildings. I respect them. But I wouldn't say that I've ever been in awe of them.

Peppered amongst our government buildings, however, you will find some modest memorials. Canada's first francophone prime minister, Sir Wilfrid Laurier, has a statue there. Laurier was no slouch. He brought both Alberta and Saskatchewan into Confederation, which is no easy feat for a French guy. He stands in a jaunty pose with one hand resting on his hip, almost as if he has stopped mid-catwalk. His statue isn't that big. If he was knocked off his pedestal, he'd be close to his real-life height. He stands facing the Château Laurier, the five-star Fairmont hotel named in his honour, which is a much bigger monument to his life. Laurier helped to secure the prime real estate for the hotel. It was built by the Grand Trunk Railway, which his government subsidized. So you could say that the hotel is more of a monument to political backscratching.

One of the first things you come across, just a stone's throw from the sidewalk in front of Parliament Hill, is a monument to the War of 1812. Of course, Canadians weren't about to let our one big victory over the United States get away without a mention. The statue depicts soldiers going every which way but forward. A Métis fighter fires a cannon in one direction. A member of the Royal

Newfoundland Regiment fires a gun in another. A woman bandages the arm of a French fighter, who may have been wounded by the Newfoundlander. A Royal Navy sailor pulls a rope that isn't attached to anything. A First Nations warrior points one way while a Canadian militiaman raises his arm in triumph, seemingly unaware that everyone else is still fighting. The seven bronze figures stand at about seven feet tall, close to life-size, underlining the very Canadian sentiment of "Okay, you're getting a statue, but don't go getting a big head about it."

Across the street, in front of the Senate building, a grouping of statues celebrates the Famous Five. These were the women who won the Persons Case, which recognized women as persons under the law and made them eligible for appointment to the Senate of Canada. The statues show the women celebrating their victory. There's even an empty chair so you, too, can be a part of the monument.

There's also a statue of Prime Minister William Lyon Mackenzie King. King famously held seances to commune with the ghosts of his mother and his dogs. There's a lot of empty space around the statue of King and I like to imagine that there are invisible statues of his mother and dogs there, too.

Peppered throughout the area, in clusters of bushes and down winding paths, you'll find statues of George-Étienne Cartier, Queen Elizabeth II and others, but, while attractive, there is nothing monumental about our monuments.

In Canada, we don't toot our own horn much. Nobody wants a thirty-foot statue of Justin Trudeau. Well, besides Justin Trudeau, that is. In Canada, we like to commemorate the things that really matter. Not the prime ministers. Not the victories. That's just not who we are. No, we prefer to honour the things that truly make us Canadian and bind us together as one nation from coast to coast to coast.

Like the Big Nickel in Sudbury. It's nine metres tall. It weighs thirteen thousand kilograms. It is sixty-four million times bigger than the real thing, so you'd need pretty deep pockets to claim it. It features an image of a smokestack on one side to honour the town's rich mining history and what I would imagine is the world's largest portrait of King George VI on the other. You'd best decide before you visit if you'd rather go to Dinosaur Valley Mini Golf or the Northern Ontario Railway Museum next, because flipping this coin would mean certain death.

The Big Nickel was the brainchild of Ted Szilva, a firefighter born to Hungarian immigrants who pitched it to the town to commemorate its centennial. But the committee rejected it, calling the plan a "Mickey Mouse operation." So he decided he would build it himself. He bought land overlooking the smelter and raised the money by selling miniature versions of the nickel through coin-collecting magazines. The city refused to offer him a building permit, so a year later the Big Nickel was finally open to the public just four feet outside of the city limits.

Today, the nickel attracts around a hundred thousand visitors a year. Sounds like a Mickey Mouse operation, all right. The Big Nickel is a mini Disneyland! I don't think of Sudbury's Big Nickel as a monument to spare change, or even mining. I think of it as a monument to what Canadians can achieve when they're too stubborn to know better.

But the Nickel is not the only oversized monument to Canadian innovation. In 1960, the Trans-Canada Highway was set to link Wawa and Sault Ste. Marie in Ontario. A Wawa businessperson named Al Turcott figured all that traffic meant a lot of potential customers zooming past his town. That could lead to a lot of extra business if he could only get those cars to stop. "Wawa" means "wild goose" in Ojibwe, so naturally he built an eight-metre-tall bird out of plaster by the side of the road. Eventually the plaster goose was replaced by a steel one, and when that rusted, they made yet another out of steel covered in bronze. The Wawa Goose became such a Canadian icon that Stompin' Tom Connors, New Brunswick's answer to Bob Dylan, even wrote a song about it. *If you should see her statue,* he wrote, *on Highway 17, you'll know that you're in Wawa, and her love song you will sing.*

One hundred thousand people visit the Wawa Goose each year, too. Maybe they're the same hundred thousand who visit the Big Nickel. They just might be, because other towns have followed suit and you can crisscross the country and visit the Big Nickel, the Wawa Goose and the Big Loonie in Echo Bay, Ontario. In Drumheller, Alberta, you'll find the World's Largest Dinosaur guarding the side of the road. She's four and half times larger than a real *Tyrannosaurus rex* and for five bucks you can climb right inside her mouth. There was also the World's Largest Hockey Stick in Duncan, B.C., once accompanied by the World's Largest Puck. The Big Apple isn't in New York. It's in Colborne, Ontario. Standing ten metres high, this tribute to apples is four times the size of any statue we have in honour of any prime minister. It attracts visitors like fruit flies.

There's a giant beaver in Beaverlodge, Alberta. A giant lumberjack's axe in Nackawic, New Brunswick. A massive moose in Moose Jaw, Saskatchewan, and a freaking big fiddle in Sydney, Nova Scotia. These are the monuments that make Canada great. They're in the heart of the country, our small towns. They show the resilience of our communities, which, like the country itself, refuse to let their size stop them. These are the things Canadians choose to celebrate.

Canada would never have its own Mount Rushmore. For starters, you'd never get the environmental approvals to blow the face off Yukon's Mount Logan just so you could stick Brian Mulroney, Chrétien and two Trudeaus on it.

Canadians would never be able to agree on whose face to chisel into it, anyway. Besides, Mulroney alone would take up half a hill just in chin. We might have a fighting chance if we agreed to a "no politicians" rule. I'd proudly stop for a picture of a mountain with John Candy, Terry Fox, Gord Downie and Anne Murray on it.

There are some Canadians that no one could argue with. In 2027, Terry Fox will replace Wilfrid Laurier on the five-dollar bill. To me, the evolution of the five is a lot like the evolution of our Canadian culture. The five used to have King George VI on it. Then we swapped him out for our own former Prime Minister Laurier. Now we are at a point in our history when we can give a spot on our money to those who have earned a place in our hearts. Moving away from the stuffy old white guys on our currency isn't a bad idea. The colours of the bills themselves shouldn't be the only diverse thing about our currency. Viola Desmond, the Black Nova Scotian businessperson who was jailed, convicted and fined for refusing to leave the whites-only section of a movie theatre in 1946, has been gracing the ten since 2018. And that's a few decades too late.

Who wouldn't want to hold on to their money when Terry Fox is on it? And imagine how great you'd feel donating a few more bucks to cancer charities when the man who ran the Marathon of Hope is on the bill? We might as well have people on our bills that bring us pride.

We so rarely get to see them these days with the current economy. Not only are we using paper money less and less, but we are all broke!

Americans love naming things after their founding father. There's Washington state; Washington, D.C.; Washington, Pennsylvania; Washington, North Carolina; Washington, Illinois; the Washington Monument; Mount Washington and on it goes. But in Canada, we have set our relationship status to "it's complicated." A statue of our first prime minister, Sir John A. Macdonald, was vandalized in 2020. Protestors threw pink paint on it during a protest at Queen's Park in Toronto. At the time, protests were erupting all over the country as Canadians were confronted with the history of residential schools. Sir John A. is regarded as the architect of the residential school system that took Indigenous children from their families, robbing them of their culture and language. Ever since his pink makeover, Sir John A.'s statue has been boarded up. The question is, was he boxed in to protect the statue or to keep Canadians from having to see him? In 2025, five years later, after many committee hearings and public consultations, Sir John A. was scheduled to come out.

For many, the statue of Sir John A. is not just a representation of our founding father; it's a symbol of oppression. For others, it's an insult to Canadian heritage to hide away our nation's first prime minister. "We're freeing

John A.," Ontario's Premier Doug Ford announced in early 2025. Ford said Sir John was being "uncancelled." So, was he a nation builder or a colonizer? In truth, a bit of both. Many of the statues of Sir John A. were erected after his death in 1891. The next batch shot up in the mid-1960s, during Canada's centenary and the same wave of patriotism that gave us our flag. But in modern Canada, we have learned more about the context we weren't taught in school. Like it or not, that colours everything, and, apparently, the colour is pink. If only we could ask Sir John A. what he thinks of how he is viewed today. If we put our ear to the plywood tomb that holds his statue, what would we hear?

Sir John A.: Hello? Helloooo? Ach, ladee. Is anyone out there? Ye boxed me in. I wish you'd gonnae no dae that! Who threw the paint? I'll gie ye a skelpit lug! Ya checky chancer! What are ye doing out there? Are ye throwing me a surprise party? Should I start counting? Ten-nine-eight-seven-six-five-four-three-two-one! Ready or nae, here I come! Hellooooo? Let me oot o' this wee box or I'll tan yer backside! I cannae even git a drink. I huvnae had a drink in years. Good thing I'm still drunk. What a fankle I'm in. You wouldna see George Washington in a bloody box, would ya? Noooo! The country he started had a bit of friggin' pride! Washington Monument. That's a nice one. Tall! Erect! White! Not that it matters. It could be any colour. I don't care. Except pink! Why pink? Is pink a popular colour in 2025? Is throwin' pink at a prime minister like wearin' black to a funeral? Is it that kind of thing?

Are there a lot of memorials to me out there? Is there a city or a province named after me? Am I still on the money? It was the ten, right? Am I still on the ten? I must be. You'd nae be so cheeky as to take the first prime minister of Canada offa the money. A statue of Laurier told me that you took me off the stamps 'cuz people kept spitting on the wrong side, but that's nae true, is it?

Hellooooo!? Is anybody out there? Oh. Wait. Bonjour! Hello? I said "Bonjour," ya French bastards! Are the French in charge? Is that it? Sneaky cheese-lovin' buggers. Okay. I have the feeling I may be gettin' the silent treatment. It's nae the first time ol' Johnny has gotten the silent treatment. I came home after a drinkin' binge once after I shite and wet meself and the front of me frock coat was covered in me own sick and the wife didna talk to me for a month.

I deserve respect! I brought this country together! I delivered it like a kidney stone into a chamber pot! So what's the big problem? Did I clear the Prairies by deliberately starving the Native population? Yes! Did I kill Louis Riel? Aye! Did I criminalize powwows? Okay, yes. Did I start the residential schools? I did! Did I . . . Oh. I'm startin' to get it.

But I built the railway! I hammered in the first spike in the Canadian Pacific Railway. The woke left said it couldnae be done. But common-sense Conservatives knew we could "strike the spike," "maintain the train" and "make way for the railway." These workers had good jobs that paid two dollars and fifty cents *a day*. A buck a day if you were a Chinese guy. Now, we didn't actually pay out a lot of that money because they kept getting blown up but the intention was there! Yes, we had to blow up about six hundred of 'em but that was the only way for us to "bring it home." Oh, wait, was that bad, too? I'm learning! I'm "putting in the work"!

Look, I know I was not wi'out controversy. I get that. My opponent, Alexander "Stop blowing up the Chinese" Mackenzie, said we gave the railway contract to a Conservative donor.

Which we did, aye. But I am a heavy drinker and cannae remember. So how can I be to blame?

They said nation-building projects like the railway couldnae be done. But I did it! All I had to do was "subscribe to the bribe," "show up to blow up" and "displease the Chinese." That's how we got on "the right track"! I don't know what the world is like in 2025, but I hope that Canada has nae sunk so low as to put lives and laws before a Conservative politician's personal ambition. Hellooo?

Okay, fine. It's a time out. I get it. You're giving me time to reflect. Or maybe you're taking the time to reflect. You know, Lincoln got a Reflecting Pool. Not that I'm jealous. I'm fine here in my reflecting box. Look, I'll be here when you're ready. I just have one ask. Next time you throw paint at me, could you please throw some whiskey along with it? Hello? Hellllooooo!? Let me oot o' this box!"

In the future, as Canada looks to choose the people and things we want to memorialize, maybe we should focus on thinking outside of the box.

Traitors

In December 2024, when Trump started making implicit threats of annexation, Canadians became suspicious of the outside world. It's not just America that put us on edge. We used to be friends with everyone. Who didn't like Canada? We were peaceful, funny and everyone's pal. Everyone wanted to sit with us at the United Nations cafeteria. But then it started to feel like people were using us. Maybe because we were pals with the popular kid, America. But then he turned on us and we couldn't tell who our real friends were anymore.

In January of 2025, Commissioner Marie-Josée Hogue delivered a report on foreign interference in Canada's electoral process. The public inquiry was called in 2023 to investigate allegations of meddling by China, Russia, India and other so-called foreign actors. The witch hunt began when a parliamentary intelligence report flagged that some members of Parliament were "witting or semi-witting" participants in foreign meddling. I'd never heard the phrase "semi-witting" before, but it did seem apt. After all, I know a couple of MPs that I'd consider halfwits. At the time, many MPs called on the government to release the names of these traitors. But were they pointing the finger to stop interference, or pointing the finger to avoid being fingered themselves? Paranoia ran wild, even for a country that had legalized weed.

However, the inquiry found no evidence of traitors in Canada's Parliament plotting with foreign governments to interfere with elections. Commissioner Hogue did express "legitimate concerns about parliamentarians potentially having problematic relationships with foreign officials, exercising poor judgment, behaving naively and perhaps displaying questionable ethics." Tell us something we don't know! Hogue found it wasn't spies that were the problem. In her report she said that "information manipulation" posed the biggest single threat to our democracy. In other words, fake news. Maybe Donald had a point after all.

There were some things to be worried about, however. She found that China "clandestinely leveraged" Canadian officials to help its "favoured" candidates win office in 2019. India, she learned, was the "second-most active country engaging in electoral foreign interference in Canada." But, in my opinion, the people that Canadians should be most worried about meddling in our affairs are Canadians. You don't need to search the dark corners of the Parliament Buildings for double agents. You don't need to bug the Chinese embassy to find evidence of someone who is betraying their country. All you must do is turn on the TV or scroll through your social media feed. They're right there, plain as day.

When the trade war started, and President Trump told Justin Trudeau that he wanted to make Canada the 51st state, most Canadians were shocked, hurt and angry. But not everyone saw this as a breach of trust. There are those among us who see every crisis as an opportunity. Like the type of people who got rich in the pandemic by hoarding N95 masks and buying stock in hand sanitizer companies. All the hand sanitizer in the world won't get their hands clean now.

Julius Caesar once said, "I love treason but hate a traitor." And with good reason. We all know what happened to him. He had one bad opinion poll and ended up a pincushion. But he has a point. Undermining authority is cool, but betrayal is unforgivable. History often chooses who the heroes and the traitors are once the battles are won. Some would look at a treasonous act as a person merely seizing an opportunity. Those people would most likely be traitors.

"Treason" is a dramatic word. It should never be thrown around willy-nilly like "hangry," "rizz" or "sus." Those words will not stand the test of time. But treason is timeless. It has a weight to it. It must be handled with care, like a loaded pistol. If it goes off at the wrong time or if it falls into the wrong hands, it can be deadly.

In Canada, treason is defined as acts against the authority of the Canadian government. This could mean trying to overthrow the government or assisting an enemy at war with Canada. High treason is more serious. That means attempting to kill the king or prime minister. High treason could get you life imprisonment. Regular old run-of-the-mill treason could get you fourteen years or an invitation to Mar-a-Lago.

The moment Trump started to talk about annexation, the *Dragon's Den* and *Shark Tank* star Kevin O'Leary ran for the border. As soon as he could, he appeared on whatever Fox News program would take him. He was desperate to get some attention from his idol.

Canadians often describe their entertainers as "Canada's answer to ______." Bryan Adams is the Canadian version of Bruce Springsteen. Rick Mercer is a Canadian Jon Stewart. And Kevin O'Leary is Canada's answer to Donald Trump. Not that anyone asked for one. He's like the wish.com version of Donald Trump. He's a little cheaper, a little smaller, not as successful. He'd be like Donald Trump without all the redeeming qualities, if Donald Trump had redeeming qualities. Trump and O'Leary are both rich blowhards who gained fame on reality TV. They are both known for terrible hairstyles. They both claim to be financial geniuses despite having run businesses that tanked. And they both tried to leverage their TV fame into political careers. Trump was successful but, thank God, O'Leary was not.

In 2017 he ran to become the leader of the Conservative Party and to defeat Justin Trudeau. He dropped out before the final debate, blaming his inability to gain traction in Quebec and his poor French-language skills. Yes, his French was terrible, but that's to be expected. To truly master French, you need to spend some time immersed in Quebec culture. To spend time in Quebec, you'd have to spend time in Canada. And, yes, Kevin O'Leary wanted to be prime minister of Canada, but he didn't want to *live* here! O'Leary was often criticized for not taking the leadership seriously. He spent much of the race in the United States, selling his own brand of wine on the home shopping channel QVC. Sounds pretty Trumpy, right?

After voters spat him out like a sensible person would spit out bad wine after tasting it, he threw his weight behind Maxime Bernier. Of Bernier, he said, "I want the DNA of my policies and objectives to survive into the general election. The candidate that best mirrors my policies is Maxime Bernier." Of O'Leary, Bernier said at the time, "O'Leary is a loser." At least O'Leary was right. Bernier was the candidate most like him because he was a loser, too. Bernier went on to form the People's Party of

Canada. It may not actually be the party of the people, but it is the party of anti-vaccination, anti-immigration voters and those who are so far right they're almost left again. In the 2025 federal election, the PPC gained just 0.7 percent of the national vote and Bernier came fourth in his own riding, losing by thirty-four thousand votes. O'Leary's political predictions are almost as bad as the financial ones made by his now defunct mutual fund company O'Leary Funds.

They call him Mr. Wonderful. They only do that because he gave himself the nickname. So is it any wonder that when Donald Trump turned on Canada, Kevin O'Leary ran to Mar-a-Lago like Jack up the beanstalk? In this version of the fairy tale, Trump was the giant and the beans were bitcoin. Before you could say "51st state," O'Leary was on Fox News telling every redneck and fundamentalist Christian watching (and likely Trump himself) that Canadians were ready to roll out the red carpet for the invading hordes. He told Fox that "Canadian people are intrigued with Trump's suggestions." I think he must have meant "person" when he said "people." Namely the only person whose opinion he usually considers, himself.

O'Leary couldn't wait to tell the Foxes in the Canadian henhouse that he had been at Mar-a-Lago and had spoken with the president himself. Which is no small feat. It's hard to be heard with your head so firmly entrenched in someone's ass. O'Leary is one of the many sycophants who pay top dollar to sit in the ballroom there waiting for Trump to shuffle by, hoping to touch the edge of his garment. Think of Mar-a-Lago as Jabba the Hutt's palace in *Star Wars*. Trump would be Jabba and Kevin would be the dancer in the metal bikini chained to his barge.

O'Leary went on to tell our invaders that Canadians were interested in the "low-hanging fruit like combining the currency." Yes, that's exactly what Canadians want, Kevin. We want Trump on our dollar. At least we could still call it a loonie. When I heard about O'Leary having dinner at Mar-a-Lago, I couldn't help but think of another dinner, many years ago: the Last Supper. Can't you just imagine O'Leary as an apostle? If they had Fox News back then, O'Leary would be right there on the news desk on Good Friday. "Look, I had no trouble turning Jesus in. The guy was a disaster. His economic policy was crucifying us. He said, 'It is easier for a camel to go through the eye of a needle than it is for a rich man to enter the kingdom of God'? Then get a bigger door! It's heaven, for Christ's sake! Look, the Romans are good people. I think Christians are intrigued by what Caesar Augustus has to say. I like Pontius Pilate. He has some great policies. He didn't want to crucify the guy. He washed his hands of it."

Kevin was speaking to the Americans, but he did have a message for Canadians. "Everyone in Canada should understand that Trump is bombastic and controversial," he said, "and they have to learn how to distinguish between the signal and the noise." *Oh, so it's not Trump's fault for threatening to annex us. It's our fault for "listening wrong." Got it.* He continued, "The noise is: 'I want to buy Canada, and I want it for a discounted price, and everybody's going to lose their sovereignty.'" *Well, that's pretty noisy.* He added, "The signal is, 'I want a strong economic union.' Don't get caught up with the noise and miss the opportunity the signal provides, is my message to Canadians."

That's like saying "Don't get caught up in the mugging. Yes, the guy in the ski mask is saying, 'I'm going to kill you if you don't give me all your money,' but that's just the noise. The signal is, 'Let's do business. In exchange for your wallet and watch, I will provide you with fifty more years of life.' That is a good deal! What an opportunity!"

Canada wasn't the only topic on the table when O'Leary visited Trump. He said he also talked about his plan to develop the world's largest artificial intelligence data centre near Grande Prairie, Alberta. As well as a proposal by a syndicate he's part of to purchase TikTok. So the noise is "I'm a traitor selling my country out" and the signal is "If I help you get Canada, you help me get TikTok." O'Leary visiting Trump at Mar-a-Lago is like going to see the Godfather on the day of his daughter's wedding. "Kevin," Trump might say from behind his desk as O'Leary grovels in tears, "someday, and that day may never come, I'll call upon you to do a service for me. But until that day—accept this app as a gift on my election day."

We had a public inquiry into the Chinese, Russians and Indians where we looked for traitors that weren't really there in the shadows. In my opinion, Kevin O'Leary did more damage to this country right out in the open on Fox News. But he wasn't the only Canadian eager to kiss the ring. Alberta's Premier Danielle Smith flew down to the seventh level of hell to join O'Leary in the heat. She said she had a "friendly and constructive conversation" with the former host of *The Apprentice*. Most conversations where one side only ever says "yes, sir" are considered friendly. Smith and O'Leary danced along the yellow brick road to see the Wizard, just like the Lion, Tin Man and Scarecrow. Without brains, hearts or courage.

At the time, Canadians were in an election. Trump's rhetoric was causing a tidal wave of patriotism that the governing Liberals were beginning to surf by standing up to Trump. After she was blessed by his Holiness the Dope, Smith spoke to American news outlet Breitbart News. They're sort of a Fox News for people who think Fox News is too liberal. Smith warned that Trump's tariffs "actually caused an increase in the support for the Liberals. And so that's what I fear, is that the longer this dispute goes on, politicians posture, and it seems to be benefiting the Liberals right now. So I would hope that we could put things on pause, is what I've told administration officials. Let's just put things on pause so we can get through an election." So, in other words, "The more you threaten our sovereignty, the less likely Conservatives are to win, so could you pretend to not want to annex us for a while so we can win and then you can do whatever you want? Thanks. Oh, is that prosecco?"

But when it comes to people who have turned their back on their country to serve their own self-interest, one name rises above the rest. When it comes to being a traitor, you could say this guy is "The Great One." When I was a kid, Wayne Gretzky was a god. The greatest hockey player of all time. His was the only hockey card that a Canadian kid would never trade. Mattel, the makers of Barbie, even manufactured a doll in his image. He made a guest appearance on *The Young and the Restless* playing himself. He was not very convincing in the part, but, nevertheless, Gretzky remained the pride of the nation. There was no one more admired. No one that Canadians were more proud of. He was our hero. These days, however, the most popular Gretzky Google search is "Wayne Gretzky traitor."

Wayne is a Canadian icon but he's an American citizen. He has lived in the States ever since 1988, when he was traded to the Los Angeles Kings and broke every Canadian's heart. But we didn't give up on him. He might live in the U.S., but he was still Canadian, right? We even awarded him Canada's highest civilian honour, the Order of Canada, in 2009. But he didn't bother to come pick it up. Maybe that should have been our first clue.

Gretzky has new friends now. One of whom is the Not So Great One, Donald Trump. Of Wayne, Trump said, "I have so many great friends. One of them is the Great One, Wayne Gretzky. I said, 'Run for prime minister, you'll win in a—it'll take two seconds.' He said, 'Well, am I gonna run for prime minister or governor? You tell me.' I said, 'Let's make it governor. I like it better.'" Hilarious. Wayne may have the Order of Canada, but it seems he takes his orders from America these days.

Canadians had been giving Wayne the benefit of the doubt for years. But things bubbled over during the NHL's 4 Nations Face-Off final between Canada and the United States in February 2025. Things had been getting heated on the ice. Canadians, enraged by Trump's comments, had begun to boo the American anthem before hockey games. This was very un-Canadian. Hockey rinks are like churches for Canucks. Anthems as revered as hymns. For us to be booing the American anthem at a hockey game meant the gloves were off like never before. Wayne didn't seem to get that. Maybe because he's been away so long, he's lost touch? Maybe it's heatstroke from playing too much golf at Mar-a-Lago? Maybe too much Wayne Gretzky Estates wine? That would do it. Whatever the reason, Wayne was not stickhandling his dual citizenship very well.

Before the puck drop in Boston, Gretzky wore a suit and tie—American honorary captain Mike Eruzione wore a U.S. jersey. This was a chance for Wayne to show his colours but he wouldn't even wear them. To add insult to injury, he gave a thumbs-up to the U.S. team as he walked to the ice from their bench. A week later, nearly fifteen thousand people had signed a petition to change the name of Wayne Gretzky Drive in Edmonton.

It wasn't just hockey fans that were upset. NDP MP Charlie Angus went off on the Great One, saying, "Wayne Gretzky should be ashamed of himself. Absolutely ashamed of himself. Don't bother coming back to Canada." It takes a lot to piss off the NDP! But just like on the ice, Wayne was not without his defenders. His wife, Janet, posted that it had broken her husband's heart to read "mean comments." Well, welcome to the internet, Wayne. It's pretty much just mean comments and cat videos.

Another great hockey player, Boston Bruins legend Bobby Orr, wrote an op-ed for the *Toronto Sun* to say how disappointed he was in his fellow Canadians. He said that he could not "understand why the 'haters' have decided to go after Wayne." No wonder Orr defended Wayne. Just like him, Bobby packed off to Florida years ago. He decided to pound sand along with the rest of the MAGA-loving Trump bootlickers who don't give a puck about this country anymore.

Orr even took out a full-page ad to help get Trump re-elected in 2020. In the ad, Orr said, "I am greatly concerned for the country in which I have raised my family" and that Trump is "the kind of teammate I want." Okay,

Bobby, you picked your team. You're an American now. Don't be telling us who we can or can't be pissed off at because guess what, Bobby, we're pissed off at you now, too!

They say Wayne Gretzky skates to where the puck is going. And apparently, that's Florida, because Wayne's been hanging around Mar-a-Lago more than Danielle Smith with an unlimited Sunwing voucher. He won't put on a Team Canada jersey, but he'll jam his hockey hair into a MAGA hat no problem. Maybe that's why broken-hearted Wayne ran to big daddy Donald to defend him, too. Some liquor stores started pulling Gretzky wines from the shelves and #GretzkyTraitor was trending on X.

So Donald came to the rescue. He posted, "Wayne is my friend, and he wants to make me happy, and is therefore somewhat 'low key' about Canada remaining a separate Country, rather than becoming a cherished and beautiful 51st State, paying much Lower Taxes, a Free and Powerful Military, NO TARIFFS, and having a Booming Economy. Wayne and Janet, his wonderful wife, love Canada, and they should only support Canada, and whatever else makes the Canadian People, and Governor Justin Trudeau, happy. He's the Greatest Canadian of them all, and I am therefore making him a 'free agent,' because I don't want anyone in Canada to say anything bad about him. He supports Canada the way it is, as he should, even though it's not nearly as good as it could be as part of the Greatest and Most Powerful Country in the World, the Good Ole'

U.S.A.!" Or, to paraphrase, "You're a good boy, Wayne! A very good boy. Daddy fixed it for you."

Yes, Wayne had his defenders, and that's the saddest part. Canadians didn't want Wayne to leave it up to his wife or Bobby Orr or big daddy Donald to defend him. They wanted to hear it from the man himself. And maybe, just maybe, he should be defending us. Gretzky famously said, "You miss 100 percent of the shots you don't take." I wish Wayne would stop hiding behind defencemen, take his own advice and take the shot.

When Premier Smith came back to Canada following her American tour, she faced a lot of criticism. She stood in Alberta's legislature to defend herself. "It's apparently treason to talk to American media personalities that we disagree with," she said. "I will not be silent. Alberta will not be silent. We will not be pushed around and called traitors."

Maybe I'm being hard on Kevin, Danielle and Wayne. But if they asked me for advice, which I can't see them doing because they only seem interested in receiving advice from Donald Trump, I'd say, "If you don't like being called a traitor, maybe stop acting like one."

A Letter Home

Lt. Clem Boone
Special Reconnaissance, USASOC
Somewhere in Canada

My dearest Britney Jean,

It has been two months since we left Fort Drum to take Canada, but it seems like two years since I last saw your pretty face. President Trump said we would take this country in just two days. Now, I have never known the president to be wrong, yet here I am, still in Canada. I promise you this: We will make Canada the 51st state by Christmas.

I know they measure stuff different up here—in metres and whatnot—but I'm starting to think that they must mark time different, too. Maybe two weeks is two months to them. I don't right know, and neither do the boys.

Morale is low. The sights we have seen, I would not dare put in this letter for how they might frighten you so. But rest assured that there is beauty here as well. The snow when it is lit by campfires. The northern lights, which are otherworldly at night. But you dare not look down, for their glow illuminates the chaos of war.

I love my country. My grandpa fought in Vietnam. My daddy in Iraq. Uncle Floyd did a tour serving as a cook at a Burger King on base at Kandahar Airfield in Afghanistan. I come from a long line of veterans who invaded and bravely retreated for their country, and I'm proud to do my part. But this just feels different. For the first time, something about invading, well, it just seems wrong.

I know that Canadians are the enemy. I do. But whenever we take the enemy prisoner, they say the sweetest things, like "Sorry for shooting at ya." They ask you, "Other than invading, have you been to Canada before?" And they give ya tips like "You have to invade Tofino before you go home," or "You should really capture Prince Edward Island if you get a chance. It's lovely this time of year."

The longer we fight and the further north we go, I can't help but feel like it's almost wrong to invade Canada.

Our commanding officer says that Canadians are just slightly warmer Russians. But I don't know. It don't sit right, somehow. Sometimes (and please don't share this with anyone, baby doll), sometimes it almost feels like I'm fighting Americans.

Now, don't get me wrong! I'm not talking about the good ol' boys from home. Not the regular folk who like to drive their F-150 down to Calhoun's saloon and down a coupla cold ones with their best girl on a Friday night. I'm talkin' more like that prof you had when you was cheerleading in college, the one from New Hampshire. You remember. The soft feller who wore them funny patches on his sports coat and done pissed himself the first time he seen a gator. New York types.

That's what Canadians remind me of. I mean, I might wanna shove them or call them something homophobic, but it just doesn't seem very Christian-like to kill 'em. Oh, dammit! I'm no good with words.

Remember Goldie? Such a good girl. She was already an old dog when we first started courting. Heck, Daddy done brought her home the same day Momma brought me home from the hospital. We grew up together. Golden retrievers are friendly by nature. But Goldie? She was something special. She never once barked at old Mr. Cunningham the postman. He used to always have the trap door of his pants torn from Miss Tammy's pit bull. But whenever he came to the door with a bill or a restraining order or an eviction notice, old Goldie would plum near lick the fingerprints right off him. And the way she'd cock her head and look at you with them big dumb eyes of hers? It was like she knew what you were saying.

It was almost as if she was human.

That's what Canadians are like. Like Goldie.

Remember when I got back from basic training? Goldie was getting too old to hunt or dig or do much of anything.

Heck, she fell asleep with her tail in the fire and didn't even howl until Daddy smelled the dog hair burning. I'd been doing drills with guns so much that I was doing them in my sleep, but when my daddy put that rifle in my hand, I felt like I'd never held a gun before in my life.

"She's your dog. Best you be the one to do it," he told me. Well, I was about to kick up a fuss and tell him that I was just a baby when he brought Goldie home. But when I looked into his eyes, I seen something I ain't never seen before. Tears.

Heck, he couldn't even finish his words. He just passed me the rifle and turned away. I ain't never seen that man cry before, Britney Jean. Not when Momma died. Not when they stole the election from President Trump. Not when he got arrested for storming the Capitol. Not even when he lost all his pension money after he invested big in Trump meme coin. Never! But he cried that day, and I done near started crying, too.

Goldie's eyes looked just like Daddy's did, full of big tears, and I could almost hear her saying "Sorry'" to me. I held up the rifle, remembered my training and said "Good girl" for the last time. That's what it feels like fighting Canadians, Britney Jean. Like putting your own dog down.

Supplies are low. We didn't expect the fight to drag on this long. We were down to the last of our rations. The other day we came across what we think is a Canadian Walmart. It's called a Zellers. I never done seen me such a depressing place. All the shelves were empty. The flickering fluorescent lights gave everything a ghostly look. It had that Russian feel to it.

Thank God Hillary Clinton didn't win the election because I've seen first-hand what socialism can bring. A sign said "The lowest price is the law." Can you imagine? Capitalism is illegal here. And believe me, baby, it shows.

We found another store called The Bay. Same thing. Nothing but empty shelves, naked mannequins and Carly Rae Jepsen muzak playing off somewhere in the distance. Creepy. How do these people survive?

I'd heard of Russian bread lines, but we couldn't even find so much as a stale slice in any of the stores we came across. We saw another empty store called Le Château. I asked our interpreter from Company D what it meant. He said it translated to "The Cat Water." Britney Jean, these people couldn't even afford to buy water for their cats. I thought of Goldie again.

Something had to be done. We had to liberate them. But we couldn't save the Canadians until we saved ourselves.

We didn't pack for winter. We were wearing OCP. That's our Operational Camouflage Pattern. It's meant to blend in with green leaves, but autumn came fast and hard in Ontario. We stuck out like a sore thumb. The only thing greener than our uniforms was our gunner, Brody. This was his first deployment, and he was itching to fight. Brody found some safety vests at an abandoned roadwork site in Toronto. The people must have known we were coming because everywhere we looked in Montreal and Toronto, we found roadworks deserted. It looked like the Rio Hato Airfield boys had done a bombing run, but we asked a local and he told us that downtown Toronto just always looks like that. We put on some orange-and-yellow vests we found layin' about, and within seconds we blended in with the foliage.

Until the next morning, when we awoke to winter. Everything as far as the eye could see was covered in thick white snow and ice. Britney Jean, I ain't never been so cold. My toes felt like they were gonna fall off, and with every step I made, I lost my boot in the snowdrifts.

To make matters worse, our electric tank wouldn't start. President Trump had replaced the M1 Abrams with the Musk 1 Cyber Tank. The Musk 1's got great agility in the field and awesome firepower—but it's not supposed to get wet. The battery got cold, and we had no way to charge it. This was just like *Black Hawk Down*, except instead of a helicopter shot down in Mogadishu we were an electric tank stuck in Ontario snow.

"I'll find us some new camo," Brody said as he slid down the ice-coated tank. Under all that ice, the flat, stainless steel panels underneath glistened in the sun just like the Costco engagement ring I bought you. "I'll be back with some chef hats or butcher's jackets or nurse costumes or something," he said as he started to run down the road.

Britney Jean, that was pretty much the last thing that good ol' boy ever said. One minute, he was looking back at us with a big ol' smile, fixin' to save us. Next thing, he was flying head over tails, spinning like one of your bras in the washing machine. That boy came down harder than a Kentucky judge's gavel on one of them Antifa persons. I jumped to help him, but my sergeant grabbed my arm. "Careful, boy," he said. "That there is black ice. Canadian quicksand."

Invisible ice, Britney Jean. They got invisible ice that covers the streets so you can't move. Up until then, we didn't have many casualties. We lost a coupla boys to gout in Quebec City. And some of our paratroopers got dropped over Newfoundland and washed up in Greenland. We were winning the war but losing the battle. They say there ain't nothing you can do to stop black ice, 'cept using salt, and damn near all of our boys got themselves high cholesterol. You know we ain't allowed no salt, baby girl.

"We can't just leave him there, Sarge," I said. "You can stay here and hide if you want, but I'm not leaving a man behind." Just then, we heard a noise I ain't heard since I was back home with you. The horn of an F-150.

"Car trouble?" A guy got out of the driver's side of the truck. He was wearing green camo just like a good ol' boy, but he didn't sound American. He walked right towards us, and the funny thing was, the black ice didn't stop him. He walked on over it just like Jesus on water.

"What's that? Electric, is it?" he asked. "Those are no good in the snow, eh? She's a beauty, though. I was just doin' a Timmies run for a double-double and thought I'd pop into the store for a two-four and a pack of darts when I saw yas. There's a Canadian Tire a few clicks back." He stopped to check on Brody. "Jesus Murphy, what a gong show. Buddy must be loaded, is he?"

Our translator was flipping through his books like crazy, but he couldn't tell us if this man was friend or foe.

Our sergeant wasn't taking any chances. He pointed his M4 carbine at the enemy and gave the order: "Stand down! Drop your weapons and surrender!"

But the man didn't flinch. "You'd have no trouble getting your moose with that, bud," he said.

"We are American forces. We are at war with your country. We are here to assimilate you as the 51st state. You will comply!" Sarge was screaming as loud as he could, but this guy just wasn't flinching.

"Sorry, eh?" he answered, lighting up a cigarette. "I don't mean to be rude and I know you're invading and all that, but your buddy's out cold. And he's bleedin' to boot, eh? No wonder he fell, with those little runners he got on. You guys want a quick rip to the hospital or wha'?"

He was right. We had no choice. We were far from home, our tank was dead and we had a man down.

Sarge aimed right for the Canadian's head. "I order you to take us for medical help, now!" Sarge always knows the right thing to do. American military superiority will see us through this conflict.

Next thing I knew I was cradling Brody's head in my lap in the back of the stranger's truck. I noticed a faded and wind-torn flag that read "F*ck Trudeau" flapping from the back of the cab. I couldn't help but wonder if this man was part of some kind of resistance. The president told us that the Canadians wanted us there, that we would be greeted as liberators. They had said the same thing about Iraq, but there, in the back of this man's truck, I felt like it was true this time.

He brought us to a Canadian hospital. My darling, I thought the Canadian stores were bad—but what I saw next chilled my heart more than black ice ever could.

The Canadian wounded were everywhere. The emergency room was packed two to a chair. They even had their sick on stretchers in the hallway. We must have been doing even better than the reports were saying. By the look of this Canadian hospital, we must have been only days away from victory. One patient told me she would have to wait six weeks just for an X-ray. Can you imagine the complete and total decimation Uncle Sam must be raining down on Canada for something like that to happen?

This is where I am writing you from now: the waiting room of a Canadian hospital. We have been making camp here for three weeks now, but I am told we will be seen soon.

At least it's warm in here. We've been living off a hot, sweet drink called a double-double and boxes of doughnut holes. The people here are welcoming, too. The man next to me tells me that he was a veteran of another Canadian conflict. He helped to shovel the city of Toronto out from under a couple of feet of snow in 1999. I asked him if he thought the war would be over soon and he told me that only we could answer that question.

"You know," he said, "the Russian army didn't defeat Hitler or Napoleon. The Russian winter did. Same thing goes for Canada. If the Canadian winter doesn't get you, Canadian health care will. One way or another, you'll eventually give up."

I asked him why everyone was still so nice to us, even in wartime.

"It's not your fault," he told me. "Donald Trump doesn't care about you, but you vote against your own self-interests because you fall for his BS. He told you he was going to bring back factory jobs and make America great again, but here you are, invading your neighbour in an electric tank.

You're just cannon fodder for the one percent. I feel bad for you."

Then he added, "Timbit?" He offered me another doughnut hole and, Britney Jean, I swear to God I never felt so gosh-darned confused. Maybe the Canadians were being so nice because they were killing us with kindness. That's a thing, you know.

The TV in the waiting room flickers to life every now and then. That's the only way we are getting any updates on our progress. But I don't know if what I'm hearing is the truth or Canadian propaganda.

The president appeared for a few minutes before we lost signal again. He said that we'd achieved the Fall of the Falls, and that America had taken control of the Niagara region. He said that Gen. Wayne Gretzky was now the warlord of the wineries there. President Trump said that American troops were marching on the Yukon from Alaska and that Russia had promised to stay out of it.

The president also told us that Quebec had surrendered and joined America, only to separate from the States moments later. The old man next to me piped up and said that we could have Quebec if we wanted it. He said that he had gotten a map of Canada tattooed on his backside so that every time he bends over, Quebec separates. I don't think he was serious. The Canadians have a weird sense of humour. I want to laugh again. I can't wait to watch some funny movies with you, like we used to back home. With your favourites, like Jim Carrey and Seth Rogen. God, I miss American movies.

The last thing the president said was that "America is going to free the Canadian people in such a bigly way—the biggest. To the United Nations and NATO and these other groups who say we must be stopped, I say to you, nothing can be further from the truth, and if you're not careful, you're going to be next, quite frankly. Do not oppose America and her allies, Russia and North Korea." How did we get here? How are we friends with Russia and at war with Canada? It don't seem right.

I told the old man that things change. I said that once upon a time Britain and Germany were friends, before the Big War. "Yeah," he said. "But which one are you?"

I don't know when I will be able to write you again, my darling. We are number 652 and the nurse says that they are now seeing number 599. Our time here is growing short. I hope we can find a place to charge our Cyber Tank so we can rejoin the fight. Are plugs different here, like in Europe? I guess we will find out soon enough.

Sorry to be writing a letter. I know how much you hate to read anything that's not a meme. But the first thing our troops did here was take out all the major telecoms: Bell and Rogers. Service has been down for days, but most Canadians haven't noticed anything out of the ordinary yet. Strange.

We have lost contact with our battalion. This letter is being sent by something called Canada Post, so I don't know when it will get there.

Ain't the stamp funny? That there is the King of England. I asked the old man here why they got an English king on their stamps if they're such a great country. Soon they will have President Trump and General Musk on their stamps like we do back home. Did you know Elon Musk is a Canadian, baby doll? True story. That must explain his funny accent. Maybe that's where the president heard about Canada. May God bless him.

Do not fret, my true love. I shall be with you soon. We shall overcome the Canadian people the same way we did the people of Vietnam, Iraq and Afghanistan—through hearts and minds.

With all my love,
Your Clem

PS: Did you know health care is free up here? We should have our next baby here.

The Last Christmas

For seventy years now, the North American Aerospace Defense Command has been tracking Santa Claus as he makes his way around the globe on Christmas Eve. NORAD is a binational military force formed by Canada and the United States. Their primary mission is to detect, validate and warn against potential attacks from air, missiles or even UFOs. But once a year, they turn their attention to one jolly old elf and nine tiny reindeer.

Kids from London, England, to London, Ontario, and from Paris, France, to Paris, Texas, check with NORAD to see where Santa is so they can be sure to have plenty of time to get out the milk and cookies before they climb into bed and dream of sugar plums. But this year was different.

Santa had just finished his visits in Canada. He was passing over the Canadian side of the Falls, flying high above the Peace Bridge as he prepared to enter American airspace. "Santa Claus is now leaving Canada and entering the United States," a Royal Canadian Air Force officer announced as he watched a red blip make its way across his screen.

"We'll take it from here," the voice came back from his American counterpart. "Attention, Quick Reaction Alert aircraft. Scramble F-16s. QRAs intercept bogey, possible hostile unidentified aircraft entering U.S. airspace. Repeat. Escort target to base. Lethal force is approved."

"Wait," the Canadian officer shouted over his headset. "That's Santa Claus. Repeat! Do not engage! For God's sake, man, it's Christmas Eve!"

"Happy holidays. I said we'll take it from here," came the reply before the line went dead. The Canadian officer watched as two more red blips appeared on his screen next to Santa. Then his screen went black. Whatever was about to happen next was not for his eyes.

At least my kids will have gotten their presents, he thought as he removed his headset and prepared to go home. Then he banished the thought from his head. Yes, security had gotten tighter over the last year. Yes, the Americans weren't sharing intel in the same way. But surely this was not what it looked like. Maybe they were just giving Santa a hero's welcome as he came to dispense a little holiday magic to the boys and girls south of the border? *Yes, that must be it*, he thought. He turned off the light at his station and headed home for the night.

High above New York, two American F-16s flanked Santa's sleigh. "Ho, h'oh no," Santa said as he tugged on his reins. The jets rocked their wings and flashed their navigation lights. "I think he wants us to acknowledge," Santa said, and waved back. Old St. Nick couldn't get a read on the pilots through their helmets and oxygen masks. Were they friendly? Naughty? "Better acknowledge, Rudolph," Santa told his trusted friend. The world's most famous reindeer swayed his head and blinked his nose to match the wings and lights of the F-16. The air force pilot banked into a slow turn, indicating the sleigh should follow. The reindeers bucked in the wake turbulence of the fearsome Viper engines. "Best do what the sons of bitches say," Santa muttered under his breath. "We have an easier time with the friggin' Russians these days."

Rudolph and Blitzen shared a glance. They both had the same uneasy feeling. There wasn't much merry about this. *I'll go down in history, all right,* Rudolph thought. *Just like Lee Harvey Oswald. A patsy full of U.S. lead.* He kicked his legs, the familiar jingle-jangle of the sleigh bells drowned out by the roar of jet engines. To his team, Santa gave a whistle. "On, Rudolph! Now, Dasher! Now, Dancer! Now Prancer and Vixen! On, Comet! On, Cupid! On, Donner and Blitzen! This part will be rough! What's next is unknown! So delete all the stuff that you have on your phones!"

When they landed, border agents turned Santa's reindeer over to the U.S. Fish and Wildlife Service. They zapped them with cattle prods for no good reason. "They speak English, you know!" Santa shouted as an agent bent him over the hood of his sleigh and restrained his wrists with zip ties. Prancer looked as though he was about to use his powerful hooves, honed by centuries of flying the globe in a single night, to cave in the head of the customs officer that was kneeling on Santa's neck. "No, no. We must be nice," Santa reminded him.

When the old man's not watching, Prancer thought. He chuckled then, knowing the old man was always watching. This was true. Santa didn't miss a thing. Sometimes, he wished he did. He had seen more naughty than nice in his life. Not that he'd ever admit it. And now he was forced to watch again, as United States border guards cut into teddy bears and stuffies and baby dolls with sharp knives. Fluff filled the air like newly fallen snow as agents from the Drug Enforcement Administration searched for heroin or fentanyl or God knows what else.

Santa had found himself in a pinch or two before but nothing like this. Even with all of the magic of Christmas, there was no way for him to get back to the North Pole, remake all of those gifts and deliver them by morning. The United States was always his last stop. At least, he thought, the rest of the world will have their Christmas gifts. But he hated the idea of even one child being disappointed on Christmas morning.

A border guard reached into Santa's sack and pulled out a snow globe. This was a special gift for a girl named Lucy. She had written specifically asking for a gift, not for herself, but for her mother. Her mother had lost her job when the assembly plant she worked for halted production due to Trump's tariffs. The snow globe showed Santa touching down on their row of houses and Lucy wanted her mother to have it to remind her that there will always be a Christmas.

The border guard shook the globe and listened to it. He watched the thick, gooey liquid swirl around the glass like a fine wine in a sommelier's goblet. He tapped the glass, thought for a moment and raised it in his hand to smash it on the concrete floor of the air force hangar. "Nooo!" Santa shouted as he threw his impressive weight from the front of his sleigh towards the sack.

"We've got a runner," he heard a voice say just before the agent changed the direction of the snow globe from the floor beneath them to the top of Santa's head. Then everything went as black as night.

When Santa came to, he was sitting in a rickety chair in Detention Room 3. He could feel the zip tie digging into his pudgy wrists and realized that someone had taken his watch. Not that he'd be able to read it with his hands restrained behind his back. The room was empty, save for a small desk, a chair, an American flag and a portrait of President Donald Trump. "Monopoly, alligator shoes, a red wagon, condoms," Santa recalled as he flipped through his mental Rolodex of childhood gifts asked for but never received. The door opened and an agent entered carrying a red folder.

"What's your name, little boy?" Santa asked, more out of habit than anything.

"You've been detained pending removal proceedings," the agent replied.

"Aren't you going to tell me your name?" Santa asked.

"I am an ICE agent, that's all you need to know." U.S. Immigration and Customs Enforcement. Santa was, indeed, in hot water. "Name?"

"Well," Santa countered, "if you're not willing to tell me your name, why should I tell you mine?"

The agent took a moment to take in his suspect. His famous fur jacket had come undone, revealing a sweat-stained white undershirt. His famous belly was not shaking, but, then again, he was not laughing now. His white beard was most definitely real, unlike the many helpers the agent had seen in countless malls. He had never interrogated anyone famous before. Most of the people he detained were poor folks just trying to get by. No one ever wanted to cough up their name on the first ask. That didn't surprise him. But even having to ask seemed silly now. Still, things had to be done by the book.

"Name?" he asked again.

"Yours is Barry," Santa said with a telltale twinkle in his eye. "Christmas 1984, you got a He-Man and a Skeletor. You asked for He-Man's castle too, but no one is that good." Santa chuckled, and the agent could see the old man's belly shaking now. He realized that he had never actually seen a bowl full of jelly shake, so he had nothing to compare it to. "You stopped believing after that," Santa said in the most sympathetic of tones. "I'm sorry."

Barry felt himself soften underneath his bulletproof vest. The past year had been hard on him. The president wanted millions of illegals deported. The department had a quota to meet of 3,000 arrests a day, up from 650 a day at the beginning of Trump's second term. He had torn families apart, been spit on and called names. In the field, agents were told to wear a balaclava to protect their identities. Now, this detainee not only knew his name but was telling him what he had wanted for Christmas in 1984. *Stop*, Barry told himself. *Just do the job. That's what you get paid for.* Barry looked back to his notes. "Name," he repeated.

"Depends on who you ask," Santa said. "St. Nicholas is my given name. That's Greek. Father Christmas is what they call me in England. I'm Sinterklaas in Holland. Père Noël in France. Some folks call me Kris Kringle, but you would know me as Santa Claus."

“That’s a lot of aliases. Which brings me to my next question,” Barry said, checking his notes. “Nationality?”

“Canadian,” Santa replied.

Canadian? This surprised Barry, but he wasn’t quite sure why. “Really?”

“Yes, really,” Santa shot back, insulted. “What’s so surprising about that? A lot of celebrities are Canadian. Michael Cera. Michael J. Fox. Mike Myers. Ryan Reynolds. Ryan Gosling. And it’s not just Mikes and Ryans, either. Lots of folks. Of course I’m Canadian. I live up north. I wear red and white, for Pete’s sake!”

“I thought you lived at the North Pole.”

“Well,” Santa replied, “Canada does lay claim to the North Pole, but technically it is not a part of any one country. Speaking of ICE, well, that’s all that it is. Ice! The true north pole is located in the middle of the Arctic Ocean, and that is international waters. It’s frozen international waters but it is international waters all the same. So you could say I am a man of the world. I don’t really belong to any one place or any one religion. I am the living embodiment of peace on earth and good will towards men . . . and women! You probably won’t like to hear this,” he said, leaning in with a wink, “but Santa’s woke.” He laughed again, this time loud enough to almost shake the room. When he was done, he wheezed and started to cough. “Ho, ho, oh, my.” His breathing was laboured now, and Barry wondered if he should cut the zip ties, but the rules had to be followed no matter who was in the chair.

"Water?" Barry offered.

"Do you have any milk and cookies?" Santa asked, with a hopeful yet bashful hint to his voice that made him sound as if he was a boy himself.

"No, sorry. Just water or coffee," Barry said apologetically.

"I'm good," Santa said, pouting.

"Do you have a passport?" Barry asked, getting back to business.

Santa stood and tried to pat his back pockets. As he did his pants slipped off his waist and, unable to tug them up again, he sat back down. "Darn belt," he chuckled. "I need to put another hole in it. My doctor has been after me to lose a few pounds. I'm pre-diabetic. All those cookies catch up with you. She has me on the Ho, Ho, Hozempic," he admitted, his cheeks turning red. "I swear on the Christmas Star that it's not for vainglorious reasons. Purely doctor's orders. Although, Mrs. Claus does say that she wouldn't mind being the one to sit on my lap for a change on New Year's. Anyway, believe it or not, my Ozempic shots are covered by my Canadian health insurance. Doesn't cost me a dime. Down here, I couldn't afford to be healthy on my salary. You know what I make a year? Nothing. Big fat zip! I'd be uninsurable down here. That's another reason why I live in Canada." Santa was beginning to ramble, and Barry began to wonder if he had something to hide. Why was he so nervous?

"Passport?" he repeated.

"Not on me," Santa replied. "It's in the sleigh."

"A visa? A permanent resident card? Anything?"

"I've never been hassled before," Santa said, and for the first time Barry could sense the frustration in his voice. "I've been crossing over the border for years. And it's not just Christmas. Me and the old lady, we drive into Buffalo for gas and a flick at the Costco and the Target from time to time. We even pop down to Florida after the busy season for a couple of days. Not this year, mind, what with all the tariff crap and the 51st state garbage." Santa froze as he realized what he'd just said. "I mean, I love the States. Look, I don't follow politics." Santa could tell he had really stepped in the reindeer droppings this time. Barry sat up in his chair and stopped taking notes.

"Let me see your phone," he said, with all the authority a badge and a zip tie can bring.

"I can't help you there," Santa said, shrugging his elbows to indicate his hands tied behind his back. "It's in my arse pocket. Help yourself!"

Barry had not expected to be frisking Santa Claus when he woke up that morning. In fact, he was hoping to get home early to tuck his son in after they checked the NORAD Santa tracker like they did every Christmas. But he was called in for a big operation. They had been monitoring a repeat offender, he had been told. A Canadian national had been slipping in and out of the country for years, moving cattle and goods without any documentation. The brass wanted to send a message to Prime Minister Carney that he needed to tighten the border, and what better time to make headlines than Christmas Eve, when the news cycle was slow and all eyes were watching.

"I'm going to have to take a look at that phone," Barry said, his hand outstretched.

"Well, bless my buttons," Santa mumbled. "I never thought I'd see the day. This is a total invasion of my privacy."

"I thought you could see us when we were sleeping and you know when we're awake," the agent scoffed. "Isn't that a little bit of an invasion of *our* privacy? Watching us sleep? You like that, do ya? Why are you watching us when we're sleeping? Why not when we're awake?"

"It's a figure of speech," Santa said shamefully. "Well, are you going to get it or not, cowboy?"

Barry sighed as he rummaged in Santa's pocket. The whole thing was made more difficult by the fact that Santa is notoriously ticklish, and his belly was shaking like a baby's rattle. He finally retrieved the device and was shocked by its appearance. "A BlackBerry Pearl?" Barry said, astonished to see that the man who made all the toys was rocking a phone from 2006.

"When you spend all day making gifts for everyone else, sometimes the last person you think of is yourself," Santa said as Barry tried to switch the ancient device on.

"Password?" he asked.

"H-O-H-O-H-O-H-O," Santa replied, with a hint of defiance in his voice even though he was complying in every way.

Barry searched through the device, but it was coming up as clean as, well, as clean as Santa's cellphone. "No Facebook. No Instagram. No email. Did you wipe this thing?" he asked.

Santa shrugged his shoulders and looked at the ground. Santa was great at many things, but he was a terrible liar.

"Wait, what's this?" Barry asked, more to himself than anyone else. His fingers danced across the keyboard feverishly and Santa became very worried indeed. "Naughty List."

"That's private," Santa said, alarmed. Few things were more sacrosanct to him than that list. Its names were privileged information, for his eyes only. "Don't you dare," he warned as Barry scrolled, his thumb rolling along the pearl with a muscle memory he did not expect. "Barry, I'm warning you."

"'Naughty,'" Barry read aloud. "'Trump, Donald J.' Well, well, well."

"Wait," Santa said, sweat starting to dampen his snow-white beard. "I can explain!"

Barry opened the door and nodded to the officers outside. Two agents rushed into the room, grabbed Santa by each arm and lifted him up. "Illegal importation of livestock, illegal importation of goods and threats against the president of the United States," Barry said coldly.

The agents hustled Santa out the door, but as he passed Barry, he stiffened, stopping the officers in their tracks with surprising strength. "Barry, I know I'm just one more Canadian being detained by you, but I want you to think of another migrant family that had nowhere to go a long time ago. They left their home in Nazareth to be counted in a census in Bethlehem. They found themselves with nowhere to stay. But the kindness of an innkeeper gave them a modest roof under which to have their child."

"You mean, an anchor baby?" Barry asked, not quite getting the reference.

"Stay with me," Santa gently urged. "Kindness. That's the true meaning of Christmas. There are children here in this facility that will have no Christmas at all. That won't ever go home again. Now, I know you don't believe in me anymore, Barry, but I believe in you. So, what say you, Barry? Will you give me the greatest gift of all? My freedom?"

Barry looked at the old man's red face. He looked to the portrait of President Trump on the wall. He wondered what he was doing. How did he get to this place? He had no ill will towards Santa or Canadians or anyone, really. All he wanted was to go home and celebrate Christmas with his family. Santa could see the turmoil on his face, and he smiled. "You're a good boy, Barry." Barry's heart swelled with the joy that only comes at Christmas.

I'm a good boy, he thought. Then he thought again. He looked back down at the BlackBerry and his thumb began the satisfying roll again.

"Now, Barry," Santa said. "Look, these things are fluid . . ."

There it was in black and white on the obsolete screen. "Gadson, Barry. Naughty."

"Take him away," he said.

"Wait! I can change that! No, ho, ho!" Santa shouted as he was pulled down the hallway. Barry straightened the portrait of President Trump on the wall and grabbed his jacket. He was going to clock out a little early tonight. After all, it was Christmas.

Epilogue

As I write this it is Canada Day. I am in St. John's, Newfoundland and Labrador, where we begin the day with our provincial Memorial Day. The National War Memorial, overlooking the harbourfront, was refurbished in 2024 for its one hundredth anniversary. The memorial had been intended to commemorate all those Newfoundlanders who would never return home. It was a place where a mother of a fallen soldier might find some closure. She would look out to sea, knowing that her son was somewhere out there on the fields of France, resting in a grave that she would never visit. But here, at this great memorial not far from where the Newfoundland Regiment boarded the ships that would take them forever away, she would have a place to mourn and remember. Last year, one of those unknown soldiers was repatriated from his grave in Europe and brought back home. After one hundred years, one lost son miraculously made his way back home after all. We do not know his name, but we do know that he is one of ours. He could be related to any one of us. He was born and died a Newfoundlander, but he was brought home a Canadian.

Hundreds of Newfoundlanders and Labradorians join me at the war memorial on this Canada Day. You can hear a pin drop as prayers are read, wreaths are laid and anthems are sung. First we sing "Ode to Newfoundland," the anthem of the old country. Then, the past remembered, we sing the new anthem, "O Canada." You can see the maple leaf wherever you look. Flying from flagpoles, on T-shirts and ball caps. I see it on the cheek of a young boy, maybe five years old. He wears a temporary tattoo of a maple leaf as he twists and turns, impatiently tugging at his mother's arm. I know that feeling. When you're a kid, things like this seem to take forever. Adults drone on and on about "lest we forget" this and "never again" that. But one day it hits you, and you realize the importance of this day. There's something about solemn reflection on how freedom is earned that makes you value freedom all the more. It's not a chore. It's an honour.

The rifles sound their salute, and the gunshots reverberate off the brightly coloured houses of Jeallybean Row. The seagulls, lazily dozing on what is a holiday even for them, suddenly take flight from the roofs of those same houses. They circle in protest, and as the sound of the gunshots fades, they are replaced with a cacophony of cawing. Necks crane for warning signs of something worse than rain. All this activity has renewed the young boy's interest, and he is bored no longer. It is now his mother who is anxiously tugging at his arm, to get ahead of the crowd as it begins to disperse.

Soon, mother and child are making their way back home, probably to fire up the barbecue and do what Canadians do on July 1. There will be no fireworks tonight, though. It's too dry for that. Never did I ever think it would be too dry for anything in Newfoundland, but here we are. The people, who moments ago had been solemnly honouring our war dead, start to settle onto the bar patios. They hug the sidewalks of downtown St. John's, and as soon as the seats are filled, pitchers of beer begin to arrive. I can't help but think that the grass is the only thing that will remain dry in this town today.

All across the city, grandparents will visit, cousins will stop by, balls may be tossed and hot dogs surely will be eaten. The day has all the markings of a lazy afternoon spent enjoying the fourth-best country in the world, according to the 2024 ranking.

Canada came in just behind the United States, in the number three spot. Japan has second place and Switzerland sits in first place. In 2023, Canada ranked second, but to be fair, it's been a rough couple of years. As I look around and see the throngs of people that surround me, it's hard not to think that we should be coming in first, though. I have my own crowd of friends and family stopping by, which means there is grass to be cut. I make the turn up one of the rolling hills of St. John's, which ensure surprisingly strong calves for every townie, no matter how big the beer gut is.

Then something catches my eye, something very un-Canadian. It is so unusual, so wrong, so out of place on today of all days that I can't help but stop in my tracks. There, parked in a small lot off Duckworth Street, is a grey Dodge Ram camper van with a sign in the front window. "Kamala Harris 2024," it reads, plain as day. It's right in the front window, where you might place a "For Sale" sign. But why? How long has this RV been parked here? Maybe they headed downtown for one too many and have been hungover since the election? Maybe this is some act of defiance, from some Canadian who, like many of us, just can't stop thinking of America, even on Canada Day?

I can't help myself. Checking over my shoulder, I lean in to take a peek through the passenger-side window. There's a Newfoundland and Labrador guidebook, a "Discover Canada" brochure, a stuffed puffin. These are obviously tourists, but why the political statement? Why try to stand out as Americans these days, and on this day of all days? My curiosity piqued, I take a walk around the camper for some clue, some sign as to why someone would be so obvious about something so passive-aggressive. That's when I noticed them. American plates. Maine. The bottom of the plate read "Vacationland," but it seemed that even people in Vacationland take vacations.

They were Democrats, so practically Canadian. But not quite. Still American. And today of all days, I am fiercely Canadian. This may just be an RV owned by two lefty Kamala fans. The type who wish they could have voted for Bernie Sanders or Alexandria Ocasio-Cortez as their candidate instead of Kamala because they thought she was too mainstream. Maybe later they planned to drive to the ocean, open the back and try some legalized Canadian weed while they blasted some Joni Mitchell over the speakers. *I drew a map of Canada. Oh, Canada. With your face sketched on it twice.*

These were most likely not invaders. Unless this was like one of those FBI surveillance vans from the movies. You know the ones. Disguised as a cleaning service or a delivery van but filled with surveillance equipment and undercover agents eating stale sandwiches with cold coffee as they wait for just the right moment to make their bust.

Maybe all this 51st state stuff was getting to me. I gave my paranoid head a shake and turned towards my house and the ridiculously steep hill that took me there. That's when I saw them: two aging hippies. The man had a grey, unkempt beard that screamed "I own an acoustic guitar." His round John Lennon sunglasses and Birkenstock sandals seemed to confirm this. And if there was any doubt, his American Folk Festival T-shirt was enough to convince any jury.

The woman with him had her white hair pulled into a tight braid. I got the sense that this was likely how she had always worn her hair. She wore a brand-new red T-shirt with a white maple leaf on it. She was either excited to be in Canada on Canada Day or she was part of the undercover surveillance team.

I hadn't yet decided, but now the tables had turned, and it was me who was keeping surveillance. It seemed that they had been watching me for at least as long as I had been watching their van. I had no reason to be suspicious of them. They, however, had been watching a man case their RV for the last five minutes. The three of us stared at one another for a moment. We were not unlike our two countries: one suspicious, the other somewhat ill at ease and frightened. But the tables had turned. I was America in this situation.

I considered my options. The first option would be for me to explain myself, say that the Kamala sign had drawn my attention and ask why they had put it there. That was what any sane person would do. It was the simplest and most honest thing to do. The choice that would lead to the least trouble.

Option number two was the more avoidant choice. I could just ignore the fact that I had been peering into their windows, wish them a happy Canada Day and wander off. This option would rely on the average person's preference to ignore an awkward situation and let things go. They would probably smile and get in their vehicle without saying a word and drive to the beach while mumbling about the nerve of that guy. They'd go home and tell their friends: "Canadians friendly? Canada safe? Ha! We caught some guy trying to break into our camper! During a ceremony for their war dead! I wouldn't go if I were you. The place isn't safe!"

The third option would be to just run. This would be my usual choice. But home was up a very long and steep hill. I would never make it. Plus, nothing looks shadier than a fifty-year-old man running away from a camper for three metres uphill before he starts to hack and wheeze and stops to take a hit from his inhaler. I could easily outrun the old guy, but the woman looked like she was a runner, possibly a vegan, definitely a vegetarian. She'd be on me in seconds and there I'd be, tackled to the ground by an American on Canada Day. I decided on option two.

"Hell of a day," I said, smiling my friendliest smile. I rolled with it, acting as if we were old friends. Neighbours speaking over a fence, which I guess in a sense we were. "'American Folk Festival,'" I said, reading his shirt. "Where's that? America?" They just stared at me, not acknowledging my question or my voyeurism. I leaned in, squinting, to read the smaller print on his T-shirt. The letters were stretched as the fabric expanded to cover what I assumed to be a tenured professor's craft-brewed beer belly. "'Bangor, Maine,'" I read. "You know, back in the 1970s and '80s we used to get our TV through Bangor, Maine." This was true, and I thought it the perfect palate cleanser. I was employing some conversational sleight of hand. I figured if I distracted them, they would have no memory of the strange man peeking through their windows. "Bangor was our TV affiliate," I continued, "so that was the local station for us whenever we watched NBC. WLBZ, right?"

The man was still wearing a somewhat stunned face. I wasn't sure if it was from the shock of seeing a near carjacking or simply because he was an American. But he gave a nod of recognition to the television station's call sign. I was in.

"There was a guy who used to host the shows there . . ." I paused. I knew the name—the TV host was a fixture of any Atlantic Canadian kid's childhood—but I felt that pretending to search for the name might endear me to them. "Eddie Driscoll!" I shouted, punctuating the moment with a finger in the air. "*The Great Money Movie*," I continued, on a roll. Surely, with skills like these, I should be working at the UN, or as an ambassador, at least. I was bringing countries together. "Eddie would show a different movie each afternoon. And a secret word would pop up. And you could send in a letter. He'd have a big rolling drum with all the postcards in it, and if he picked your name and called and you knew the secret word, you could win money! I loved it. One time, a neighbour was called but they weren't home. I never knew such excitement as I did when I saw Eddie Driscoll pull a Newfoundland phone number out of the drum and call it. 'One ringy-dingy,' he said. 'Two ringy-dingies.' After three ringy-dingies the jig was up and he moved on, but for three shining ringy-dingies, Newfoundland was on the map!" I stopped, my story told. Surely these people would be gobstopped, running into a random Canadian who knew their hometown so vividly, without ever having been there? Now the stories they relayed when they got home would be favourable.

But they did not look convinced. They shared a glance and then the woman spoke up. "Were you just looking in the windows of our RV?"

I turned to look up at the hill. Maybe I could make it four metres before having to resort to my inhaler? "Yes," I admitted. "I was, but I can explain."

"The Kamala sign, right?" the old guy asked. It seemed I had not been the first to leave nostril prints on their passenger-side window. "We put that there because of the American plates," he said rather sheepishly.

"We didn't want people up here to think we were Trumpers," the woman added. The two of them averted their gaze slightly, like two kids who had broken a window with their ball. I sympathized with them. I was about to say that they didn't have to worry about stuff like that here. That we were Canadians! That we were above such petty biases. Then I remembered that I had just been caught circling their car like a bomb-sniffing dog.

"We put that up in the window everywhere we go," the old guy explained. "We don't want anyone to vandalize the camper or think we are assholes, so we dug around the shed and I came across the sign. It's not like we were super into Kamala or anything. Or Biden, to be honest. We were more voting for anyone but Trump. Just wish we had a better candidate."

"Bernie?" I asked.

"We love Bernie!" the lady exclaimed.

Nailed it. Their predicament reminded me of the COVID days, when Atlantic Canada had its own bubble. Any vehicle with out-of-province plates was shunned. One with American plates would have been avoided as if it carried the plague, which it most likely did. But now the virus was a thought. COVID had been replaced with MAGA and Canadians were spurning the very idea of an idea. These seemed like good people. They shouldn't have to wave a white flag just to watch us wave ours. I asked them if they'd had any trouble.

"No," she told me. "People have been nice. But if we're at a campsite, sometimes, after a few beers, they rant about Trump a bit." I assured them that this wasn't necessarily because they were in the company of Americans. Most Canadians do go on and on about Trump when they are drunk. I asked them why they chose Newfoundland, and they told me they had always wanted to drive up through the Atlantic provinces, but never as much as since they had seen the musical *Come from Away* on Broadway a few years back. The show tells the story of 9/11 through the eyes of the townspeople of Gander, Newfoundland, a small town that welcomed seven thousand stranded airline passengers. It struck me that these two folks had wanted to visit Newfoundland after seeing a show about Newfoundlanders welcoming Americans and now didn't feel welcome as Americans in Newfoundland.

America is more than its leader. The ties that bind the U.S. and Canada cannot be severed by any one person or even the millions of people that voted for that person. I was reminded of my Great-Aunt Tillie. She was shipped off to live with relatives in the 1920s when her father died. She and her sisters went "into service" for families in New Jersey. They married and started lives there. Once a week, my parents would call us out to the telephone chair to say hello to this phantom relative we would never lay eyes on in the flesh. She had that big, loud, slow-talking American voice that we only ever heard on the TV set. But she still had many of the sweet Newfoundland affectations that you heard from any other relative of her generation. "How are you, my love? Are you being a good boy, my ducky?" her voice would bellow down the line, a strange mix of here and there.

Every birthday and Christmas, without fail, a card would arrive with an American stamp. "Dear Mark, here's a little greenie for you." Greenie. That's what she called the American money she would send as a gift. She'd lived as an American for three times as long, but she still saw the colour of the bills there as something foreign. Tillie is long gone now, but I reconnected with her granddaughter on Facebook. She has a collection of the letters we sent south of the border, and I still have all of the ones Tillie sent north. Yes, we are a sovereign nation. No, we will never become the 51st state. Yes, Trump is an asshole. But the tea bag is in the water now, and there's no separating the water from the tea. We are different in the same way.

The couple took the Kamala sign down from the window, and I told them that they didn't really need to do that here. They told me thanks, and they felt more comfortable with it up there. They bid me farewell and got back in their RV. That didn't sit right with me, so I tried a different tack. I tapped on the glass, and the old guy put his window down with a smile. "I'm having some family over to the house for Canada Day," I offered. "It's just straight up that hill. If you'd like you're more than welcome to come up and have a hot dog and beer. Meet some Canadian cousins?"

I felt I had done my part. If they wanted a little *Come from Away* magic, I would give it to them, right then and there. They looked at each other as if they had been propositioned with either drugs or sex. "No, thanks," the old guy said, as his window shot back up. I don't know if he thought he would be taken to a POW camp for prisoners of the trade war, but he started his RV like he was in the Indy 500 and they sped off down the street. I guess there are still some differences between Americans and Canadians after all.

I made my way, wheezing, up the hill. Happy to be on this side of the fence.

Acknowledgments

First of all, I would like to thank Donald Trump for making me so angry that I wrote this book. Thanks to Kristin Cochrane, Scott Sellers and everyone at Penguin Random House Canada for giving me another chance to write. I'm honoured to be associated with them and I still get a rush whenever I see that little penguin near my name. I'd also like to thank my literary agent, Michael Levine, and all hands at Westwood Creative Artists for sound advice given in a calming tone. I owe a lot to my editor, Laura Dosky, for agreeing to have me turn around a book so quickly. Her ability to roll with the punches has been a saving grace.

Big thanks to Tracey Jardine and the gang at *22 Minutes* for their health and eternal kindness.

I'm grateful to my wife, Melissa, for putting up with all my grumblings about having to write a book, even though it was my own darn fault.

And finally, a giant thanks to all the wonderful Canadians who read my words or watch my shows. You've given me the gift of living a dream without leaving home. I would never want to live anywhere but here in Canada.